The real Catherine (Kate) Hewitt has been found! For those who love and a great mystery, this book is for you. Through impeccable research, historian Jeff Harding and his research associate Mary Stanford Pitkin have answered the enduring questions surrounding General John Reynolds's fiancée, Kate Hewitt. In this very readable book, the reader will discover who she was, what happened to her after Reynolds's untimely death at Gettysburg and the location of her final resting place. A dual biography of General Reynolds gives context to the ill-fated relationship. But this is no dry historical recitation! Harding takes you with him on a fascinating journey of discovery as he uncovers clues, which he deftly weaves into an engaging story. The outcome is satisfying and a little bit shocking.

—SUE BOARDMAN, *historian, licensed battlefield guide, former Leadership Program director for the Gettysburg Foundation Leadership Program and coauthor of three books:* Elizabeth Thorn of Gettysburg: The Wartime Caretaker of Evergreen Cemetery; The Battle of Gettysburg Cyclorama, A History and Guide *and* The Gettysburg Cyclorama: The Turning Point of the Civil War on Canvas.

Gettysburg—its history, its memory, its characters—has a near totemic significance for millions of people. Now Jeff Harding has written a book that will further delight this group. Blending new research with a keen knowledge of history and a detective's instinct for the meaning behind the facts, Harding provides an engaging chronicle of the relationship between General John Reynolds and "Kate" Hewitt. But more than anything this is a story, written with insightful empathy, of Kate herself, including new information about her life's continuing journey following Reynolds's death at Gettysburg. Rudyard Kipling said, "If history were taught in the form of stories it would never be forgotten." After reading Harding's book I will be remembering the John and Kate romance, and appreciating Kate, in new ways. Jeff Harding has given us a wonderful story that adds to our understanding of the history, the memory and the characters of Gettysburg.

—LAWRENCE TAYLOR, *U.S. ambassador (retired) and co-founder of the Gettysburg Leadership Experience*

A mystery that has puzzled Gettysburg historians for years has been solved! The fate of Kate Hewitt, the secret fiancée of General John Reynolds, is now a compelling true story of love, sacrifice and redemption. Jeff's meticulous research (along with Mary Stanford Pitkin) has uncovered facts never before seen and has unveiled the truth of the Reynolds/Hewitt relationship.

—MICHAEL A. RILEY, *historian and author of* "For God's Sake Forward!": General John F. Reynolds, USA

The ill-fated saga of John Reynolds and Kate Hewitt has long fascinated those interested in the Battle of Gettysburg. We have wanted, for many years, to know more about the mysterious Kate. Thanks to Jeff Harding and genealogist Mary Stanford Pitkin we now know why Kate did not want to be fully discovered, yet her story continues to amaze us. This is a carefully documented chronicle of love, loss and triumph—and why the Civil War, with its myriad participants, continues to fascinate us.

—DIANA LOSKI, author and editor of The Gettysburg Experience *magazine and author of* The Chamberlains of Brewer *and* A Gettysburg Collection, Biographical Treasury

The sudden death of General John F. Reynolds and the dramatic effect it had on the love of his life, Catherine "Kate" Hewitt, has long been a simple anecdote about the Battle of Gettysburg. Author, historian and licensed battlefield guide Jeff Harding has gone one step further to unearth the story of this tragic and heartbreaking relationship and chronicle the story of love that bloomed only to come to a sad end on the battlefield and beyond.

—JOHN S. HEISER, historian, National Park Service (ret.)

Jeff Harding's Gettysburg's Lost Love Story *closes the book on the answer to a question that has eluded Civil War historians for generations. It also offers an intriguing look at Kate Hewitt's life before John Reynolds and begs the question as to what Reynolds knew of her early life when he proposed to marry her.*

—FRED VEIL, great-grandnephew of Charles Veil (General Reynolds's orderly) and former executive director of the Sharlot Hall Museum in Prescott, Arizona

Jeff Harding has penned an interesting and thoughtful portrayal of the lives of General John Reynolds and his fiancée, Kate Hewitt. Although much is known about John Reynolds, little has been known until now about the life of Kate Hewitt. Carried out with the assistance of Mary Pitkin, Mr. Harding's dogged pursuit of evidence reveals heretofore unknown details about Kate Hewitt's life and its trajectory following the death of John Reynolds, painting a clear picture of her persistence and resilience even under daunting circumstances. This highly readable story will be of interest to historians and non-historians alike.

—JANET MORGAN RIGGS, President Emerita, Gettysburg College

GETTYSBURG'S
L O S T
LOVE
STORY

The Ill-Fated Romance of
General John Reynolds and Kate Hewitt

Jeffrey J. Harding

Foreword by Wayne E. Motts,
President and CEO of the Gettysburg Foundation

THE
History
PRESS

WEN,
I TRUST YOU WILL
ENJOY THIS STORY!
BEST WISHES,
JEFF

Published by The History Press
Charleston, SC
www.historypress.com

Front cover, bottom: Dale Gallon's *Reynolds*, by Dale Gallon (www.gallon.com);
top: Kate Hewitt. *Courtesy of Katie Cleaver*; John Reynolds. *National Portait Gallery,
Smithsonian Institution*; *back cover, top*: Engraving, "The Fall of Reynolds." *Library
of Congress. Back cover, inset*: Image of rings by Dale Gallon. *Harding Collection.*

First published 2022

Manufactured in the United States

ISBN 9781467151597

Library of Congress Control Number: 2021950578

To the memory of my mother and father.
I miss you both—every day.

CONTENTS

CONTENTS

A NOTE ON THE TEXT

Y ou will note that I refer to General Reynolds more often than not as John Reynolds, General Reynolds or simply "Reynolds," especially regarding the military aspects of his life. However, in referring to Catherine Hewitt, I typically use either her entire name or the informal "Kate." To me, this feels appropriate, as referring to Kate simply as "Hewitt" feels much too stilted. On occasion I refer to General Reynolds as "John," especially when discussing matters relevant to personal matters, such as his relationship with Kate or his correspondence within the Reynolds family. Without meaning to be presumptuous, I find this my natural inclination, and to me this method of referring to both individuals seems to humanize the narrative without leaving one with any notion of bias. Regarding John's sisters, to whom he frequently wrote, you will see Mary Jane referred to as either "Jane" or "Jennie," Catharine referred to as "Kate," Harriot referred to as "Hal" and Eleanor referred to as "Ellie." This is the manner in which John referred to each. Their given names are used in any related reference listings.

No man died on that field with more glory than he, yet many died, and there was much glory.
—BREVET MAJOR GENERAL HENRY J. HUNT, USA,
chief of artillery of the Army of the Potomac,
reflecting on the death of General Reynolds at Gettysburg[1]

Not all sacrifices are made on the battlefield.
—ANONYMOUS

FOREWORD

More than thirty years ago now, the dean of Gettysburg historians, Lieutenant Colonel Jacob M. Sheads (AUS ret.), left me with an unfinished research project. The "Colonel," as he was affectionately called, was my mentor. A native of Gettysburg, he could trace his lineage far beyond the date of the battle to the early history of Gettysburg. Colonel Sheads was a World War II veteran, the high school history teacher at Gettysburg High School, a Gettysburg National Military Park ranger, a licensed battlefield guide and the very man who escorted our thirty-fifth president, John F. Kennedy, and his family over the battlefield in 1963. The Colonel had a favorite story, a mystery he was always intrigued with, the story of what happened to Catherine M. Hewitt. She was the fiancée of Union major general John F. Reynolds, who died in the Battle of Gettysburg on July 1, 1863. Colonel Sheads told me before his death, "Wayne you need to find her grave and what happened to her." For years, not just me, but others have looked to discover what happened to this young woman. Reynolds's biographer Michael A. Riley and I spent a number of years working to find out what really happened to Catherine Hewitt and to locate her final resting place. We even assisted Civil War artist Dale Gallon with a painting related to the subject titled *The Last Promise*, which was released in 1997.

In 2005, a small booklet was published related to Hewitt and Reynolds. As it turns out, the fate of the Catherine Hewitt profiled in that small work was not that of John Reynolds's fiancée. In other words, it is not the correct Catherine Hewitt.

In short, I could not fulfill Colonel Sheads's wish to discover what happened to Catherine Hewitt or where her remains rested, but in 2020 my longtime friend and fellow guide Jeff Harding and his research associate genealogist, Mary Stanford Pitkin, finally solved this mystery. Sheads died in 2002, but he would have been proud to know his number one Gettysburg story and mystery was finally put to rest. Like many stories from our past, this one is far more interesting than anyone could have possibly envisioned. Catherine Hewitt went "missing" in 1868, and now 154 years later, her true story is finally revealed. Through painstaking research, the use of unpublished and newly digitized sources, Jeff Harding, for the first time, has woven a narrative that details the intertwined lives of Catherine Hewitt and John Reynolds.

I am so proud that after all these years, thanks to Jeff and Mary's research and Jeff's labors in conveying this story in book-length treatment, we not only have the answer to Gettysburg's most enduring love story and, in my opinion, its number one mystery, but also a complete understanding of *Gettysburg's Lost Love Story: The Ill-Fated Romance of General John Reynolds and Kate Hewitt.*

—Wayne E. Motts
President and CEO of the Gettysburg Foundation
Licensed battlefield guide, Gettysburg National Military Park

PREFACE

Why *Gettysburg's Lost Love Story: The Ill-Fated Romance of General John Reynolds and Kate Hewitt?* Why did I choose to focus on this story when the Battle of Gettysburg resulted in tens of thousands of tragic stories? Though there is no single answer to these questions, I shall endeavor to offer both a broad brush and a personal perspective on the reasons why.

In the grand scheme of things, the Battle of Gettysburg presents historians with any number of stories of heroism, tragedy and sacrifice. And inarguably, the story of Major General John Reynolds's untimely death at Gettysburg combines all three of these circumstances. But when the general's secret engagement and the uncertain fate of his fiancée, Kate Hewitt, are considered, an increased level of mystery and intrigue comes to the fore. Add to this the poignant story of Kate promising John she would enter into a religious life if he were to be killed during the war, and you have all the makings of what one would normally look to find in a novel. Sadly, this story was true.

Then there were the lingering uncertainties surrounding Kate's life. Where was she actually from? Who were her parents and the supposed brother who had reportedly disowned her? What were the circumstances surrounding her relocating to California at a relatively young age? Why did she move there, and what type of life did she lead there? What inspired her to leave California? How did she meet John? When did they become engaged? And after losing John in the war, what became of Kate? Was she able to live up to the promise she had made to John? And if not, what actually happened to her? How did she live out the rest of her life?

In considering all of these questions, it seemed as though many elements of the story surrounding the ill-fated romance of General John Reynolds and Kate Hewitt were still missing. In fact, key portions of the story appeared to be scattered to the four winds and in essence "lost" to history. And that, as much as anything else, has tugged on historians' curiosities for over a century and a half. I was one such historian.

Interestingly, the very first stop on the Gettysburg National Military Park battlefield tour map, stop one, is the site where General Reynolds was killed. When I took my oral exam to become a licensed battlefield guide at Gettysburg National Military Park, the first "story" I told on my examination tour was the one about John and Kate. And ever since then, on virtually every tour I've given, I've shared this story with my guests. To me, this story humanizes the overall tragedy of the battle. And humanizing the calamity at Gettysburg is necessary, as the numbers are mind-numbing. The titanic clash of armies at Gettysburg resulted in a total of 51,000-odd casualties (killed, wounded, captured, missing), with estimates of those dying from the battle (both immediately and afterward) ranging from 10,000 to 15,000. After the battle, approximately 21,000 wounded soldiers were left behind by the armies in Gettysburg, a town of 2,400 people. Even today this would be overwhelming, but in 1863 it was an utter calamity.

Tom Desjardin's wonderful book *These Honored Dead* puts these numbers in perspective—in 1863, one out of every 200 persons alive in the country at the time fought at Gettysburg. Today, if we had a battle this large (relatively speaking), it would involve nearly 1.5 million soldiers, and somewhere around 100,000 human beings would die in three days (the length of the battle). Can you imagine? It is certainly hard to get your mind around the enormity of the disaster.[2]

That is why human-interest stories prove so beneficial. These stories help those of us who lead tours at Gettysburg bring meaning to the staggering numbers. These stories also show how the tentacles of tragedy and sacrifice reach deep and long on the homefront, affecting spouses, parents, siblings and family members for generations. In the case of John Reynolds, this tragedy and sacrifice affected not only his family but his fiancée, Kate Hewitt, as well.

The pain of losing someone we love is something almost all of us can relate to, in one way, shape or form. And those of us who have felt the pain of loss related to war and horrible events, like 9/11, know all too well the depth of the grief that stems from lives taken long before they should have ever been lost.

So you ask, "Why John and Kate, why *this story*?" The simple answer is because this story brings together heroism, tragedy, sacrifice, mystery, intrigue, sense of loss and perseverance. But it is also because this story allows us to convey the story of the Battle of Gettysburg in a fashion that helps individuals remember what happened at Gettysburg. The story of John and Kate, and her ultimate fate, add color to the overall story of a battle that would otherwise be black and white. As guides, the honor of speaking for those who can no longer speak for themselves is never lost on those of us who are blessed enough to serve as licensed guides at Gettysburg. It is, without a doubt, a great privilege to do so.

Jeffrey J. Harding

ACKNOWLEDGEMENTS

This book would not have been possible if not for the efforts of genealogist Mary Stanford Pitkin, to whom I offer my heartfelt appreciation. Mary's findings proved invaluable in unfolding the true story of Kate Hewitt. Mary found the genealogical family tree that proved so crucial to Kate's story. Mary and I first revealed some of this information in the August 2020 issue of *Civil War Times*. Mary also discovered the newspaper account that hinted at Kate's "colorful" experiences in California, and she conducted an exhaustive search for Kate's parents and her brother. My everlasting thanks to Mary for sharing my passion for uncovering Kate Hewitt's life story.

A sincere thank-you also goes out to Liz Anibal Werner, the great-granddaughter of Joseph B. Pfordt, the man once married to Kate Hewitt. Liz generously provided access to the Pfordt family Bible, which proved invaluable in documenting the final chapter in Kate's life. Liz also joined the effort to place a proper gravestone for Kate Hewitt in the Pfordt family lot at Saint Agnes Cemetery in Albany, New York.

My gratitude extends to all those who have come before me in researching the story of Kate Hewitt and John Reynolds. This work stands on the shoulders of many, especially Edward Nichols, Mary Maloney, Wayne Motts, Mike Riley, Kalina Ingham Hintz and Marian Latimer.

I offer my deep appreciation to John Fulton Reynolds Scott III, Mary Scott and Carol Eberhardt, the great-great-grandchildren of John Reynolds's sister Catharine Ferree (Reynolds) Landis. Each kindly offered their support and assistance for my research in many ways, especially in providing a detailed description of John Reynolds's West Point class ring. Likewise, my most sincere appreciation extends to Katie Cleaver (and her husband, Peter Crabtree), the great-great-granddaughter of John Reynolds's sister Lydia Moore (Reynolds) Evans. Katie's mother, the late Anne Hoffman Cleaver, dedicated much of her life to the preservation of the Reynolds family history. Katie kindly allowed me unique access to historical documents, family photos and extraordinary artwork created by her mother. Among these items are an extremely rare image of Kate Hewitt and a remarkable etching that depicts members of the Reynolds family and Kate Hewitt on the battlefield at Gettysburg not long after John's untimely death. Both are published here for what is believed to be the first time.

When looking for someone to champion their efforts, a person could not be more fortunate than to have an individual like Wayne Motts in one's corner. Longtime licensed guide colleague, renowned Civil War historian, former CEO of the National Civil War Museum (NCWM), president and CEO of the Gettysburg Foundation and a loyal friend of over twenty-five years, Wayne Motts provided 360-degree support to me, from start to finish. Wayne's assistance was unflinching, enthusiastic and nothing short of critical to the success of this work.

I was also blessed by having historian, publisher, author and former Gettysburg licensed battlefield guide colleague Diana Loski to consult with on this effort from beginning to end. Diana carefully reviewed my manuscript, and she kindly translated a rare document written in French that I had received from the Eden Hall archives. This document shed invaluable light on Kate Hewitt's Eden Hall experience. Diana's counsel and assistance throughout this process was a Godsend.

Renowned artist Dale Gallon and his wife, Anne, deserve my sincere thanks for their enduring interest in the unfolding of the story of Kate Hewitt and John Reynolds. Dale's magnificent lithograph titled *The Last Promise* stands as a lasting tribute to the love once shared by Kate and John. Dale generously created an artist's impression of John Reynolds's West Point class ring for this book. This image is the first-ever likeness of the Reynolds ring, and as such it represents a treasure in and of itself. It is published here for the first time.

I would also like to thank historian Mike Riley, author of the outstanding monograph of John Reynolds *"For God's Sake, Forward"*, for consulting with me on various aspects of my research and for taking the time to review my manuscript. No one knows more about John Reynolds than Mike Riley, and I am humbled by his kindness and generosity.

A number of phenomenal archivists proved invaluable to this effort, including Scott Keefer, provincial archivist at the Daughters of Charity; Sister Carolyn Osick, provincial archivist, and Michael Pera, assistant archivist at the Society of the Sacred Heart Archives (SSHA); and Christopher Raab, associate librarian for archives and special collections at Franklin and Marshall College's Marin Library of the Sciences. Each of these individuals provided critical assistance in responding to my sundry requests for documents and images while also offering unique insights relevant to my research.

I owe numerous guide colleagues, staff and historians at Gettysburg National Military Park and the Gettysburg Foundation a debt of gratitude for their support and assistance. Sue Boardman generously provided access to several amazing photos from her personal collection for this book, and she kindly reviewed my manuscript as well. Others who assisted include Barb Finfrock, Dr. Charles Fennel, Mike Kwolek, Britt Isenberg, Christopher Gwinn, R. Gregory Goodell and former GNMP chief historian John Heiser, who also took time to review my manuscript. My appreciation also extends to noted historians John Hennessy, R.E.L. Krick and Jim Burgess, all of whom kindly offered their insights and expertise on the portions of this work relative to their areas of expertise. Special thanks also go out to Ronald S. Coddington, editor and publisher of *Military Images* magazine, and contributing editor Elizabeth A. Topping for lending their expert assistance and photo analysis skills with regard to two of the extant photographs of Kate Hewitt included herein. My deepest appreciation also extends to Sam Small of The Horse Soldier for his kindness in allowing me to publish John Reynolds's brigadier general of volunteers commission. My sincere gratitude to my associates Lawrence Taylor and Janet Morgan Riggs for reviwing my manuscript; I am humbled by their kindness. My thanks also go out to Meagan Huff, curator at Fort Vancouver National Historic Site, who provided a plethora of information about the fort and access to an extremely rare image of John Reynolds and the Third U.S. Artillery; Gina Bardi, reference librarian at San Francisco National Historic Park Research Center, who kindly assisted me in obtaining key information on the Pacific Mail Steamship Company and the SS *Golden Age* as well as the Port of San Francisco during the mid-nineteenth century; James Scott, librarian and archivist at the Sacramento Public Library, who provided key pieces of information relating to Kate Hewitt's life in Sacramento as well as details on available period photos; Tom Wentzel, Lititz Moravian Congregation Archives, who kindly provided a wonderful image of a rare telescope used during John Reynolds's time at the "Beck School" in Lititz; and Cory Van Brookhoven, Lititz Historical Foundation, for providing a rare image of the school itself.

My heartfelt gratitude to Fred Veil, great-grandnephew of Charles Veil and former executive director of the Sharlot Hall Museum in Prescott, Arizona, who kindly reviewed my manuscript and, along with the museum staff, provided access to two extremely rare images that appear in this book. My thanks also to: Kim Chantry, Philadelphia Historic Commission, who was extremely helpful in obtaining information on and photography of the former residence of John Reynolds's sister Kate in Philadelphia (the home on 1829 Spruce Street where John's remains were brought to after his death and where the family first met Kate Hewitt); Kelly Grimaldi, associate director of St. Agnes Cemetery in Menands, New York, who provided crucial support with regard to information contained in the cemetery internment book and Kate Hewitt's burial; Holly Hayes, administrative assistant, Historic Saint Mary's Church in Albany, New York, who kindly located the transcribed church records for the marriage between Kate Hewitt and Joseph B. Pfordt; John "Jack" McEneny, William "Bill" Carroll and Peg Harrigan of Albany, New York, all of whom provided invaluable assistance to me regarding Kate Hewitt's life in Albany; Albany historians Carl Johnson and Don Rittner, both of whom kindly shared their insights; Linda Williams, Tioga County Historical Society, who provided important information on Benjamin Hewitt, Kate's brother, as well as images of Owego; Peter Gordon, town historian of Owego, who lent his expertise on the history of both the Village and the Town of Owego. My appreciation also extends to Nathan Pease, Kevin Shue, Marianne Heckles and Heather Tennies of LancasterHistory; West Point librarians Suzanne Christoff and Casey Madrick; West Point curator of art Marlana Cook; Sister Betty Ann McNeil and Sister Margaret Ann Gainey of the Daughters of Charity; W. Douglas McCombs, Albany Institute of History & Art; Michael Hillman, History Emmitsburg Historical Society; the staff at the South Coastal Library, in Bethany Beach, Delaware; and Lisa Tassa of the Calvert Library—the world's most extraordinary librarian.

My sincere thanks go out to everyone at The History Press, most especially acquisitions editor extraordinaire J. Banks Smither. Working with him, copy editor Abigail Fleming and the entire team of experts at The History Press has been a true pleasure from start to finish.

To all of the unnamed others who graciously responded to my requests for information and assistance, I sincerely appreciate your kindness. If by chance your contributions to my research are not reflected here, please trust that I may yet find a related project for which I might use such information.

On more of a personal note, there are a few friends and family to whom I owe a special thank-you.

I offer my appreciation to my lifelong friend John Roberts for his assistance in researching Catholic religious medals, former colleague and friend Glenn Richards for his photo analysis assistance and my friends Dr. Robert Noel and historian Tom Foley, both of whom were kind enough to review my manuscript and offer key suggestions.

I also owe a lifelong debt of gratitude to the late Dr. James Therry, who was an exceptional professor of U.S. history at Prince George's Community College in Largo, Maryland. At a key point in my life, Dr. Therry recognized there was much more to this seventeen-year-old than met the eye, despite my strolling in tardy to the first day of class in less than proper college attire. Dr. Therry's subtle but gentle rebuke stirred something in my soul. And ultimately it was he who renewed my passion for history, a passion that had been sown many years earlier but forgotten amid myriad teenage distractions. The lessons he taught me in class, and most especially those he taught me about life, shaped my future and made me a better person. Dr. Therry's lovely wife, Brenda, a woman of tremendous intellect in her own right, survives him and was kind enough to review my manuscript and make a number of beneficial suggestions.

Regarding men who influenced my life, my father is second to none. He set an amazing example not only as a father to me and my siblings but as a devoted husband to my mother as well. And it was he who opened my eyes to sacrifices made by the members of U.S. military. Drafted into the U.S. Army right before the end of World War II, he was fortunate in that the war ended before he saw combat. But he lost a number of friends and classmates in the war. And he never forgot the effect their deaths had on him and their families. At times, my father's gift of gab surfaced, and when it did, he was in his glory. I suppose he passed that trait on to me as well, and I thank him for that gift, as it certainly helps me be a better guide and teacher, despite the fact that it caused a lot of heartburn for my elementary school teachers.

Above all, there is one person to whom I owe my love of history—my mother. Aside from being the most wonderful mother a son could ever have wished for, my mom planted the seeds of interest that led to my passion for history. As a fourth-grade teacher in the state of Maryland, mom taught Maryland history each year. Every summer, she and I visited historic sites in the state. To this day, I enjoy very fond memories of our travels together and all the sites we visited. And I will never forget the songs we sang during our travels, especially the chorus from our favorite song, "Those were the days my friend, we thought they'd never end, we'd sing and dance forever and a day…" Thankfully, she lived long enough to see some of the fruit born from the seeds sown in my formative years.[3]

Last but certainly not least, I offer my love and heartfelt appreciation to the remarkable women in my life: my wife, Teresa, and my three daughters, Amber, Crystal and Brandi. Each of my daughters supported my efforts with kind words of encouragement, and I could not be prouder of each of them for the amazing women they have become as citizens, wives and mothers. The eight spectacular grandchildren they have given my wife and me, along with our wonderful sons-in-law, are among my life's greatest rewards. Regarding life's blessings, my wife and her marriage to yours truly for over forty-one years stands atop all others. Her decades spent by my side speak volumes with regard to her patience, understanding and commitment to vows expressed so many moons ago. Throughout the research and writing of this book, she tirelessly (most of the time) listened to my tales of woe and success as the tide of potentially beneficial research ebbed and flowed. In the process, she came to know Kate and John better than she ever expected or perhaps wanted to. Regardless, I thank her for her understanding of my passion for researching this story and writing this book. I regret the time lost that we might have spent together while I was hard at work on this book. Hopefully, there is time enough in our lives for me to make up for moments we might have shared. Rest assured, I will endeavor to do so.

INTRODUCTION

T here is something in this book for everyone. Indeed, it was written for casual readers and historians alike. For casual readers, almost everything you read will be new, whether it pertains to John Reynolds, Kate Hewitt or both. In many ways, this is the ideal circumstance, as you come to this book with no preconceived notions and no misunderstandings relative to this story. With this, you should revel in the unfolding of this story, enjoy its mystery and intrigue, anguish over its tragedy and appreciate the heroism, sacrifice and perseverance it reveals.

As far as historians are concerned, this work presents a cornucopia of new information. Recently discovered primary sources reveal previously unknown details on Kate Hewitt's life ranging from shocking revelations relating to the years she spent in California to the true story of her ultimate fate. The last subject is no small matter, as Kate's true fate and circumstances surrounding her death had either been unknown or misunderstood for nearly 160 years. This work clarifies information regarding Kate's actual place of birth as well as the existence and identity of her brother. Moreover, even the smallest of details relating to Kate do not escape scrutiny, such as the proper terminology relating to her time with the Daughters of Charity. (For example, in the Daughters of Charity community, she definitely would not have been called a nun but rather a *sister*.)

Meanwhile, an accompanying overview of John Reynolds's life and service before and after meeting Kate Hewitt provides context to their story. Recently unsurfaced documents reveal details pertaining to the voyage on which John first met Kate. This book also provides a fresh analysis and discussion of when John and Kate likely became engaged. Here, you will also find details pertaining to the rings they exchanged and clarification regarding the type of religious "medals" found on John's remains. Moreover, recently discovered information pertaining to Kate adds a new dimension to the understanding of John's and Kate's relationship and their secret engagement. Finally, there is one additional "golden nugget" here—this work presents, for what is believed to be the first time ever, an artist's impression of John Reynolds's actual 1841 West Point class ring.

John Reynolds's life has been well documented. He was from a family of letter writers and wrote many letters as a young adult and throughout his military career. These letters are rich in detail, both professional and personal. Fortunately, his family saved his letters, and his descendants donated these letters to Franklin and Marshall College in Lancaster, Pennsylvania. Edward Nichols's landmark biography of John, *Toward Gettysburg*, relied heavily on these letters, and his book remains the definitive work on John's life—it really is a masterpiece. More recently, historian Mike Riley's monograph on Reynolds, *"For God's Sake, Forward!"*, added invaluable insights into Reynolds's life and career. Numerous other articles relative to episodes in John Reynolds's life echo and supplement these works. With this, deciding what information to include on John was akin to trying to figure out how to get a sip of water from a fully charged firehose. In the end, much of what appears in this book pertaining to John Reynolds stems from the aforementioned sources. That said, this work also contains additional information pertaining to Reynolds from both primary and secondary sources.

Prior to the publication of this work, much of Kate Hewitt's life story had remained a mystery. Though a number of authors and researchers have delved into her history, important details of her life remained uncertain. With this, the love story surrounding John and Kate seemed incomplete. Like a great work of art that had been inadvertently cropped, pieces of the "canvas" that conveyed important information relative to their story were missing. Unlike researching John's life, the issue for Kate was not "culling the herd" in order to decide what information to include but rather finding any new or pertinent information to add to her story. While the information on John Reynolds flowed like water from a firehose, information on Kate Hewitt came like drips from a slowly leaking faucet. Fortunately, though, a few of those "drips" proved remarkably enlightening. Regardless, this book attempts to fill in as many of the missing pieces of Kate's story as possible so that the overall story of the relationship between Kate Hewitt and John Reynolds can be not only viewed in context but also fully understood and appreciated.

Kate Hewitt would probably have led a life of total obscurity if not for her relationship with John Reynolds. Famously, he was the first general and the highest-ranking officer killed at the Battle of Gettysburg. But because of his death, their romance has taken on mythical proportions. Certainly, her engagement to John was the central event in her life. Yet there is more to her story. Kate's life represents a story of amazing perseverance. If ever there was a story of someone refusing to give up, this is it. In addition, Kate's life experiences offer unique insights into the struggles of a single woman left to fend for herself in mid-nineteenth-century America.

In the end, this book combines the story of Kate Hewitt's life with that of John Reynolds in a manner that provides you with an enhanced understanding of each individual's life while also detailing Kate's relationship with, and engagement to, John Reynolds. With this, I trust you will enjoy *Gettysburg's Lost Love Story: The Ill-Fated Romance of General John Reynolds and Kate Hewitt.*

1

JOHN

GETTYSBURG

Forward men forward!

By the time Major General John Reynolds approached the battlefield at Gettysburg during late June 1863, he was forty-two years old. By then, he had dedicated twenty-six years of his life to the military. During his tenure, he had seen considerable action and fought heroically during the Mexican War, experienced brushes with Indians and returned to his alma mater as commandant of cadets. As spring turned to summer in 1863, the war that most expected to end quickly had raged on for over two years, and there seemed to be no end in sight. During these two-plus years of war, John Reynolds's star had risen sharply. He fought valiantly at Mechanicsville and Gaines' Mill during the Peninsula Campaign. And in the words of Reynolds biographer Edward J. Nichols, his defense of Henry House Hill during the Second Battle of Bull Run was nothing short of "brilliant." All the while, Reynolds had advanced through the ranks from brigade to division and finally corps commander. As the Gettysburg Campaign unfolded, he served as a wing commander of several corps. Having proven his leadership and battlefield prowess on numerous occasions, he had won the admiration of friends and foes alike. In short, John Reynolds seemed destined for greatness. President Abraham Lincoln recognized all of this when he offered Reynolds command of the Army of the Potomac on June 2, 1863. Demurring, Reynolds settled into his role as wing commander. Throughout his years of dedicated service, John Reynolds had experienced numerous brushes with death. Placing himself in harm's way, he often presented an easy mark for sharpshooters, yet miraculously, he had escaped unscathed. In considering Reynolds's good fortune, one mesmerized soldier went as far as to say Reynolds led "a charmed life"; another, commenting on one of the general's narrow escapes, attributed his survival to the fact that "his hour had not yet come."[4]

Physically, John Reynolds's bearing impressed nearly everyone. One soldier indicated he was "tall, fully six feet in height, with dark hair and eyes, erect carriage, whether on foot or horseback; and while inclined to slimness, possessed a commanding figure. He was a superb horseman, and was so much at ease in the saddle as to be able to pick up from the ground at full speed a silver ten-cent piece and to dismount while vaulting with his hands on the pommel." Another said he sat his horse "like a Centaur, tall, straight, and graceful, the ideal soldier." As a leader, he knew when to be firm and when to use tact, all of which drew admiration from those he led. One underling officer who encountered Reynolds while trying to select a proper place to direct a column of troops into bivouac (temporary camp) commented, "Had he chosen to do so, he could have given me orders, as the senior officer present, but with a gentle courtesy he accomplished his purpose without that, and to reassure me gave his name and rank in this delicate way. I shall never forget his pleasant smile as he returned my salute after thanking him for his suggestion." It seems Reynolds had mastered the art of building respect and commitment not only through leading by example, during combat, but also by knowing how to use his rank subtly when the situation warranted. One volunteer likely put it best when he said, "He was the very beau ideal of the gallant general."[5]

Toward the end of June 1863, John Reynolds gradually moved the left wing of the Army of the Potomac toward the portion of the Mason-Dixon line that marked the border between Maryland and Pennsylvania. Reynolds's wing (First, Third and Eleventh Corps—some thirty thousand men) moved as part of a larger movement as the Union army fanned out on a thirty-mile front (east to west) in search of the Confederate army. Though Robert E. Lee and the Confederate army had "stolen" a march on the Union army and entered Northern territory in mid-June, they had been caught off guard by the approaching Union army due to a startling lack of intelligence. When on June 28 Lee finally realized the Union army was hard on his heels and much closer than he anticipated, he began to consolidate his army. He did so by ordering his forces to march quickly toward his base of operations near Cashtown, Pennsylvania (about eight miles west of Gettysburg). At the time, elements of Lee's army were as far away as York, Pennsylvania, thirty miles to the northeast, and Harrisburg, Pennsylvania, thirty-eight miles to the north. As a result, large portions of the Confederate army were approaching the Union army from the northeast, north and west.

As his troops moved earnestly toward Lee's location, between June 29 and the morning of July 1, Reynolds's left wing of the Army of the Potomac formed the leading edge of the entire Union army. As the two goliath armies, numbering some 163,000 Union and Confederate troops, groped for each other, the ten roads leading to Gettysburg began to draw the armies together. Soon the crossroads town of approximately 2,400 inhabitants formed a bull's eye, and with this, the stage was set. Each of the ten roads became potential fuses, any one of which could catch fire and explode, figuratively, in a moment's notice. Any such detonation would result in a titanic clash of armies the likes of which had never before been seen on the North American continent. These were the circumstances into which John Reynolds led his forces during the early morning of July 1, 1863. It was a situation ripe for disaster.

Sunrise on the morning of July 1, 1863, saw John Reynolds organizing the First Corps, vanguard of his wing command, for the day's march toward Gettysburg. The day was not particularly warm by typical early July standards for south-central Pennsylvania. Based on local weather observer Professor Michael Jacobs's measurements, the temperature may not have reached eighty degrees. Still, the day was uncomfortable based on the dew point (estimated at seventy-four at 2:00 p.m.), particularly in the afternoon and evening. One of Reynolds's staff members commented on his discomfort, "We moved off at 8 a.m., the weather still being muggy and disagreeable, and making the roads very bad in some places." Localized showers and misty rains from the previous day caused some roads to become difficult. Meanwhile, cloudy skies and an ever-so-slight southerly breeze prevailed throughout the day.[6]

The First Corps units were moving to Gettysburg in support of cavalry commander John Buford's troopers, who had picketed the western and northern approaches to Gettysburg the previous evening. In accompanying the lead division of the First Corps, it wasn't long before Reynolds heard the distant sounds of battle. Moments later, he encountered one of Buford's couriers. The horseman had been sent by Buford to inform Reynolds that a portion of Robert E. Lee's forces was advancing on the town from the west, along the Cashtown Pike. This early morning dispatch alerted General Reynolds to the fact that John Buford's cavalry, which was located less than five miles away, had engaged the enemy. Instructing the First Corps to hurry their approach, Reynolds earnestly set out with his staff for Gettysburg.[7]

Arriving in Gettysburg at roughly 9:30 a.m., Reynolds sought out cavalry commander John Buford. Stories conveyed by those on the scene vary as far as the place of their encounter. In one version, Reynolds located Buford perched in the cupola of the Lutheran Theological Seminary. The picturesque seminary grounds were located just west of the town, set squarely on a prominent north–south ridge overlooking the western approaches to town. The cupola offered Buford a commanding view of the entire area. Seeing Buford, Reynolds famously quipped, "What's the matter, John?" Buford's equally if not more famous retort came quickly, "The devil's to pay." In the vernacular of the rugged trooper, this meant his men were hard-pressed and they needed help quickly. In another less fanciful version, Reynolds found Buford somewhere around the eastern fork of McPherson's Ridge, just beyond the seminary. Eminent Gettysburg historian Edwin B. Coddington points to this version as the most reliable inasmuch as it was conveyed by Reynolds staff.[8]

Early in the morning on July 1, an outpost of Buford's troopers stationed along the Cashtown Pike, about three miles west of town, fired on approaching Confederates. Buford's goal was to delay the Confederates as long as possible and prevent them from seizing the high ground just east and south of town. But once fired upon, the men in butternut and gray were only too happy to return the favor. Buford's engaged forces numbered some 2,700, but 1 out of every 4 troopers was responsible for holding his fellow cavalrymen's horses; thus Buford's effective force numbered approximately 2,000. The attacking Confederate force approaching from the west on the morning of July 1 numbered approximately 2,800 effectives with another 3,000 or so soldiers (infantry and artillery) close by and another 6,000 within striking distance. Though most of Buford's troopers shouldered single-shot breech-loading (nonrepeating) carbines, allowing for more rapid firing than the rifled muskets employed by most infantry, the infantrymen's weapons allowed for much greater distance and accuracy. In any event, by the time Reynolds encountered Buford, the beleaguered blue-clad troopers had fought an admirable delaying action against the ground-pounding Rebel infantry for nearly two hours. And though Buford's men had done just about all they could do to save not only

This image depicts the most popular interpretation of the meeting of General Reynolds and General Buford on the morning of July 1, 1863. Primary documentation supports both this interpretation of their meeting as well as at least one other interpretation of where they met. Buford and Reynolds, *by Dale Gallon (www.gallon.com).*

the town but also the high ground, their main line of defense was about to unravel.[9]

After briefly riding out to assess Buford's position, Reynolds took immediate action. He quickly assigned one of his staff members to deliver an urgent message to General George Gordon Meade, commanding officer of the Army of the Potomac. He instructed the courier to ride as fast as possible, even if the hard ride were to "kill his horse." He sent messages to Generals Howard and Sickles, the other corps commanders of his wing command, to come to Gettysburg "with all dispatch." And then he hurriedly rode back to meet and urge on the lead elements of the First Corps, the first division, as they approached Gettysburg. Numbering approximately 3,500, the first division would have to hold until the remainder of the corps and lead elements of the Eleventh Corps could arrive, and that would not be any sooner than 11:00 a.m. But at least the first division's arrival would better the odds both numerically and in pitting infantry against infantry.[10]

In a matter of moments, the van of the First Corps arrived on the scene, and Reynolds was in the midst of the brewing maelstrom. It was about 10:00 a.m. Arriving just as Buford's right flank threatened to falter, he sent a brigade of his infantry (about half the division) in to bolster their position. Next, he placed an artillery battery in position to defend the middle of the Union line of defense. Finally, Reynolds turned his attention to the vulnerable and increasingly threatened left flank of Buford's tenuous line of defense.[11]

Seeing the approach of another brigade of reinforcements from the first division must have heartened Reynolds beyond description. Here, in perhaps the most critical moment of the morning fight along McPherson's Ridge, Reynolds found the group that was arguably the First Corps' most hardened and stalwart veterans—the First Brigade of the First Division of the First Corps of the Union Army—the Iron Brigade. These steadfast troops had earned their moniker in blood on the slopes of Maryland's South Mountain ten months prior during the Antietam Campaign. Seconds likely seemed like hours to Reynolds as he directed these men into action with the words, "Forward into line at the double quick!" Reynolds's orderly Private Charles Veil said of Reynolds, "Where ever the fight raged the fiercest, there the general was sure to be found, his undaunted Courage [sic] always inspired the men with more energy & courage. He would never order a body of troops where he had not been himself, or where he did not dare to go."[12]

And true to form, as the actions escalated near an outcropping of trees known as Herbst's Woods (adjacent to and at times also referred to as a portion of McPherson's Woods), Reynolds continued to lead from the front just as he had done on so many other battlefields. Though Reynolds typically refrained from quixotic behavior, pitched battle often brought out his visceral inclinations. This time was no different. As Reynolds observed enemy forces earnestly approaching, he urged on a regiment of the brave Wisconsin men of the Iron Brigade with the words, "Forward men forward for God's sake and drive those fellows out of those woods." As he sat astride his trusted black steed Fancy, Reynolds realized his men were hard-pressed to the front and on their left flank. Seeing that their fate was in question, he turned to look for the remaining regiments of the brigade. Then, at that critical moment, Major General John Fulton Reynolds was struck in the back of the neck by an enemy bullet. He immediately fell to the ground.[13]

Reynolds's trusted orderly Charles Veil dismounted immediately and rushed to Reynolds's aid. Unable to locate the source of the general's wound, Veil saw only "a bruise over his left eye." Moments later, Veil and

Throughout his military career, General Reynolds exposed himself to danger as he led troops into the heat of the action. On the morning of July 1, 1863, his efforts in leading the Second Wisconsin into position proved crucial to holding off the Confederate attack, but this time his penchant for leading from the front cost him his life. Iron Brigade Forward *by Mark Maritato, image courtesy of artist.*

staff members Captains Mitchell and Baird joined in the effort to carry the general away from danger. As the rescuers carried Reynolds toward safety, they thought they heard the general exhale, so they stopped and attempted to provide him with a drink of water, to no avail. Soon after it was found that the fatal bullet had indeed entered the back of Reynolds's neck, near his right ear. John Reynolds, fearless leader and gallant soldier, was dead.[14]

The highest-ranking officer killed at Gettysburg, John Reynolds died during the opening salvos of a battle that would see some fifty-one thousand casualties, with estimates of somewhere between ten and fifteen thousand lives lost as a result of the battle. When John Reynolds was killed, it was definitely a calamity for the Union army. General Meade was said to have stated he would "rather have lost twenty thousand men, for the country's sake, than Reynolds." Reynolds's death was most certainly a tragedy of untold proportion for his family. But his death marked an even greater heartbreak for someone else.[15]

As Major General John Fulton Reynolds's remains were examined, a silken cord was found around his neck. Attached to this cord were two

"The Fall of Reynolds," as depicted by artist Alfred R. Waud. This engraving was derived from a drawing by Waud. The drawing was likely based on eyewitness accounts. *Library of Congress.*

Catholic items, a cross and a heart. On one of his fingers was a small ring inscribed with the words "Dear Kate." Closer examination of John Reynolds's remains also revealed the fact that the general's West Point class ring was missing. And lastly, two mysterious letters were found in his valise, both signed "Kate." (The details surrounding Reynolds's death, and the items detailed here, are confirmed in letters from his sister Jennie and his aide-de-camp William Riddle. See chapter 10, note 115 and chapter 15, note 162 for source information and further discussion.)

But who in the world was Kate? As it happened, no one knew. Soon enough, that would change.

2

JOHN

CHILD OF PRIVILEGE

One of thirteen children…

Though he was orphaned relatively early in life, John Reynolds's father, John "Lancaster" Reynolds, made quite a name for himself. The elder Reynolds operated as a successful publisher and politician. As the owner and editor of the *Lancaster Journal*, the town's Democratic-leaning newspaper, everyone who was anyone knew his name. Moreover, the elder Reynolds ran in prominent circles that included his good friend, senator and future president James Buchanan. In fact, he often carried out local business for the erstwhile Buchanan while the latter was in session with the U.S. Congress. The connection proved to be one of critical importance to Reynolds. But that came later.[16]

Meanwhile, John Fulton Reynolds of Gettysburg fame likely received his first military influences from stories shared by his mother, Lydia Moore Reynolds. (John also had a sister named Lydia, and John's aunt, his father's sister, was named Lydia as well.) Lydia's father, Samuel Moore, once served as a captain in the Continental army and saw action during the Battles of Brandywine and Germantown. Sharing a strong patriotic lineage likely served to stir the martial spirit among the Reynolds boys, as two of the four who survived to adulthood would ultimately enter military service.[17]

John Fulton Reynolds was born in Lancaster, Pennsylvania, on September 21, 1820. His birth marked the fifth in the fast-growing Reynolds family. Over the course of twenty-one years, John Reynolds's mother gave birth to thirteen children. Sadly, three died in infancy and one other child died when only four and a half years old (Anne Elizabeth). However, nine offspring survived, including Reynolds's older siblings, Sam, William and Lydia, as well as his younger siblings, James, Jane (Jennie or Mary Jane), Catharine (Kate), Harriot (Hal) and Eleanor (Ellie).[18]

With such a large family, it comes as no surprise to find that the Reynolds home was among the town's largest. Life in Lancaster provided plenty of distraction from daily chores for the Reynolds children, as the town of nearly ten thousand inhabitants boasted everything from wagon and railroad manufacturing to plentiful surrounding woodlands and waterways. All of this likely combined to satisfy the yearnings for adventure among the Reynolds family youth whether it be fishing, hunting or investigating all the town had to offer. In other words, during the early nineteenth century, Lancaster proved an ideal place for a child to grow up.[19]

Regardless of the many distractions the town provided, education remained of utmost importance in the Reynolds family. Evidence indicates young John Reynolds thoroughly enjoyed the years he spent while boarding at a private school in nearby Lititz, Pennsylvania. The popular school was operated by John Beck. Entering the school in the fall of 1833 at the ripe age of thirteen, John wrote home often. And each time he did so, it was in a favorable light. In a letter written to his sister Lydia just before the Christmas break, he waxed on and on about the wonderful school and the recent lessons on "the virtues that adorn a good mans [sic] character." He summed up his state of mind by indicating, "I think I never passed the evenings happier and more to my advantage than I have done since the 1st of November."[20]

It is also interesting to note that Reynolds, in his youth and as an adult, typically expressed warm sentiments at the end of his letters, such as "Your Affectionate Brother" and "much love to Mother and all the family." His love of family gatherings at Christmas also shone through in statements like "tell me how we are to come home at Christmas." These traits were destined to continue whether Reynolds wrote from West Point, Mexico (during the Mexican War) or any other far-flung duty stations. The love of family never left him, and it likely shaped his desire to someday marry and raise a family of his own. Meanwhile, at Lititz, of all the requisite lessons to which he was exposed, it seems Reynolds especially enjoyed learning horseback riding. John Reynolds was young, but his love of horses proved an enduring one.[21]

The three-story building with dormers in the middle of this photo shows John Reynolds's birthplace and his boyhood home in Lancaster, Pennsylvania. *Courtesy of Lancaster History, Lancaster, Pennsylvania.*

By the summer of 1835, Reynolds was off to another school: Baltimore's Long Green Academy. His letters from Baltimore seem to indicate he was nowhere near as enamored with Long Green as he had been Beck's school. Nonetheless, Reynolds returned home within a year and completed his education at the Lancaster County Academy.[22]

Left: Lititz Academy, founded by John Beck. *Courtesy of the Robert "Sketch" Mearig collection.*

Right: This telescope was used by students of the Lititz Academy during the time John Reynolds attended the school. *Courtesy of the Lititz Moravian Congregation.*

Reynolds's biographer Edward Nichols notes one particular character trait John Reynolds developed during his formative years. Per Nichols, Reynolds maintained a keen interest in his own fitness, even to the point of being "preoccupied with his health." Whether at home or away at school, Reynolds always seemed concerned with maintaining his physical well-being. This was a trait that would hold him in good stead as he inched ever so closer to a life where the demands on his strength and vigor would be severe.[23]

By 1836, big changes were afoot in the Reynolds family as John "Lancaster" Reynolds's commitment to a close friend very likely shaped young John Reynolds's future. One primary source indicates the elder Reynolds had agreed to act on behalf of his friend Robert Bird Coleman should Coleman predecease him. This commitment included not only managing Coleman's business interests but serving as a guardian for his children as well. True to his word, when Coleman passed away the elder Reynolds sold the Reynolds family home in Lancaster and moved the family to Pennsylvania's Lebanon Valley in order to fulfill his obligation.[24]

The increased responsibility of caring for several additional children apparently created a strain on the Reynolds family finances. With this, the attractiveness of an expense-free West Point education came to the fore. And it was a perfect fit for John Reynolds. His admiration of older brother William's military career with the U.S. Navy certainly played a role as well. William, thanks to the good graces of family friend Senator

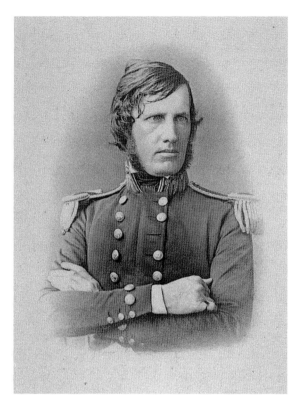

Lieutenant William Reynolds, John Reynolds's second-oldest brother. This view of William is estimated to be from the 1840s, likely after his return from the historic U.S. Exploring Expedition of 1838–42. *Courtesy of Katie Cleaver.*

Buchanan, had previously been appointed a midshipman in the navy. Edward Nichols speculated on why Reynolds might have opted for the army over the navy, citing his love of horses and also his fondness for hunting. Per Nichols, Reynolds might have seen an opportunity to hunt various types of game at duty stations across the country as another advantage to army life over a life spent largely at sea. Another factor influencing Reynolds's decision might have been stories shared by his brother concerning the austere nature of life as an aspiring naval officer. Life as a midshipman also left much to chance, promotion-wise, while a West Point education, though challenging, offered a clear-cut path to becoming an officer.[25]

In any event, during the winter of 1835–36 the elder Reynolds sought a West Point appointment for fifteen-year-old John Reynolds through his friend Senator Buchanan. Both father and friend were left a bit embarrassed by the response from Secretary of War Lewis Cass informing the senator that Reynolds's September birthday precluded his ability to meet West Point's requirement for all those admitted to be sixteen years old as of June of the year of admittance. Not to worry. The following year, the effort was renewed, and in March 1837 John Fulton Reynolds wrote to the secretary of war to accept his appointment, indicating, "I therefore hasten to assure you, that with great pleasure, I thankfully accept the appointment." Reynolds's letter was dated March 6. Ironically, on March 7 a new secretary of war was seated. His name was Joel Roberts Poinsett. Poinsett had been the nation's first minister to Mexico years earlier, and he is largely credited with introducing the plant that bears his name to the United States. But it is the Mexico connection that holds the irony, as John's West Point education would lead directly to his rise to prominence in the army during the United States' Mexican War of 1846–48. Of even keener interest, though, was the fact that as John prepared to embark on the road to his future, something that would profoundly affect his life, but in a totally different way, had already occurred not far from the place he would spend the next four years of his life.[26]

3

KATE

OWEGO ORPHAN

A mysterious beginning…

Catherine "Kate" Mary Hewitt was born on April 1, 1836, in Owego, New York, located along the banks of the Susquehanna River in Tioga County, New York, not far from the Pennsylvania border. In light of future events, it is interesting to note that Owego rests along the same line of longitude (76 degrees) as Lancaster, Pennsylvania, and the two towns are separated by only about two hundred miles. Like John Reynolds's father, Kate Hewitt was likely orphaned at an early age. Supposedly, she was the daughter of Richard Hewitt and his wife, Jemina (or Germina). The source for this information seems reliable enough, as it is none other than Kate Hewitt. In fact, she provided this information in official documentation on at least two occasions. However, herculean efforts to locate her "family tree" have borne little fruit. This is made all the more perplexing by the fact that, per information also provided by Kate, we know her parents' names. At least we *think* we do. But in the absence of corroborating documentation, we are left to wonder if young Kate Hewitt picked the names out of thin air.[27]

Unlike John Fulton Reynolds, who had a well-documented family ancestry, Kate Hewitt did not. Reynolds was a tragic war hero from a prominent family. There is a plethora of information pertaining to his life: official army records, voluminous family correspondence, a landmark biography and numerous secondary sources. Kate Hewitt appears not to have been from a famous family, no family letters survive and secondary sources pertaining to her life are typically left to rely on the scant

Owego, N. Y. and Susquehanna River

An overlook of the village of Owego. Though likely depicting the village sometime after Kate's departure, most of this landscape shown here would have likely been familiar to her. *Courtesy of the Tioga County Historical Society.*

information. In short, finding primary source documentation pertaining to her life represents a formidable challenge.

Fortunately, Kate Hewitt also made mention of having a brother. And that brother, Benjamin Hewitt, *does* appear in numerous pieces of official primary source documentation (various census reports and so forth). Moreover, on at least three occasions he is mentioned in period newspapers. Taken together, this evidence definitively links him to Kate Hewitt. And perhaps the most fortunate part of all this is that Kate's brother lived in the same town in which Kate was supposedly born—Owego, New York. Thus, this connection appears to confirm the birthplace Kate Hewitt listed for herself on the same documentation in which she gave her parents' names.[28]

So if Kate Hewitt told the truth about her birthplace, why would she have lied about her parents' names? Most likely she didn't. Yet as mentioned previously, an exhaustive effort undertaken by an extraordinary genealogist failed to identify Kate's parents in any federal or New York State census records.[29]

In considering all of this, only a few explanations make sense. Either Kate Hewitt's parents died shortly after she was born, or somehow they

Kate Hewitt's brother Benjamin Hewitt lived most of his life in the Owego area and once served as the South Owego postmaster. He is buried in the South Owego Cemetery. *Courtesy of the Tioga County Historical Society.*

missed being accounted for in census reports. (This is certainly possible if they moved and perhaps missed the census, in both coming and going, before they died.) Or maybe Kate inadvertently recorded the wrong names for her parents. Then again, perhaps Kate's parents died when she was too young to remember their names. With this, she might have been provided with incorrect names by either well-meaning family members or friends of the family.

Regardless, it appears as though Kate Hewitt was an orphan, though, in the absence of ironclad documentation, we can never be absolutely certain. However, everything we know from existing documentation supports this contention, including the fact that she indicated she was an orphan. This evidence comes to us through reliable documentation in the form of an 1863 letter preserved by the Reynolds family—more on this later.[30]

In the end, there are many unanswered questions pertaining to Kate Hewitt's formative years. That said, we *do* know what Owego was like at the time of Kate's youth. But before providing those details, it is important to clarify that Catherine "Kate" Mary Hewitt was from Owego (no *s*), not Oswego, New York—some researchers have made this mistake. And she is absolutely not from Stillwater, New York; that was an altogether different woman also named Catherine Hewitt.[31]

Thanks to the kind staff at the Tioga County Historical Society (TCHS) and the historian for the town of Owego, we know quite a bit about Owego around the time Kate would have lived there. The following is a compilation of what the aforementioned sources described:

> *Growing up in the mid-nineteenth-century village of Owego would not only have placed Kate in Tioga County's seat of government, but in a bustling and vibrant community. The village of Owego, nestled within the surrounding town of Owego, was then, and is now, located on the banks of the Susquehanna River. It was a booming Village with large lumbering and transportation industries. With this, Kate would likely have been exposed to all sorts of river traffic to include flatboats carrying lumber. As the county seat, Owego boasted a courthouse along with a requisite number of surrounding lawyers' offices. And the town could also be proud of its two weekly newspapers, a post office, fire department and even an opera house.*

A 4430 Main Street, Owego, N. Y.

This image of Main Street, taken a number of years after Kate left the Owego area, provides a good representation of what the street surroundings would have looked like during Kate Hewitt's formative years. Though the "Great Fire" of 1849 destroyed many of the once familiar wooden storefronts, the building on the left with the columns (a hotel) survived the fire and would have been familiar to Kate. *Courtesy of the Tioga County Historical Society.*

Owego's Front Street follows the Susquehanna River and was once a Native American path. *Courtesy of the Tioga County Historical Society.*

Several well-established churches filled out the landscape along with the Owego Academy and several "female seminaries." And finally, the arrival of the railroads in the late 1830s and into the 1840s ultimately led to a new level of prosperity to the town, including three- and four-story hotels, but most of this came in the 1850s. If Kate Hewitt did in fact spend her youth in Owego, Kate would have seen a number of beautiful homes along Front and Main Streets.[32]

Of course, all of this leaves us wanting more. For instance, where did Kate Hewitt go to school, and how long did she stay in Owego? Again, documentation is scarce. But available primary source documentation indicates Kate did have an excellent education. In fact, one reliable account states she was "highly educated" while another describes her as having a "refined" mind. And as we will see later, her written word supports this contention.[33]

As indicated by the TCHS, there were numerous schools in Owego during Kate's time there. And at least one, the Owego Academy, was highly regarded. Unfortunately, primary source records for the academy during the years Kate Hewitt might have attended (based on her age) are incomplete. Of those records that do exist, none list Kate as a student. At least three other female schools served the area during Kate's youth, but no rosters from these schools survive. It is interesting to note though, that one local school instructor was none other than Belva Bennett McNall. The name might not ring a bell, but this was the same woman who, after her remarriage, became known as Belva Ann Lockwood, the famous women's rights advocate. Whether or not she taught in Owego during Kate's formative years remains uncertain. Another of the local schools boasted the instructional talents of local artist Thomas LeCler, who would become known as one of the nation's most famous artists.[34]

The Owego Academy provided a quality education for young women and men and represented one of the most desired schools in the Owego area during the time Kate Hewitt lived in the area. *Courtesy of the Tioga County Historical Society.*

Suffice it to say, the details of Kate Hewitt's family and her early life remain uncertain. But we do know she had conclusive ties to Owego, New York. And knowing this, if nothing else, gives us some idea of what her surroundings might have been there. But most importantly, all evidence points to the fact that Kate, along with her brother Benjamin, likely experienced the life of orphans at a relatively early age. Such circumstances can often be, at the very least, difficult. At times they can be dreadful. We don't know Kate's exact circumstances. But what we do know from her later life is that whatever circumstances shaped her, the result was a woman of immense internal fortitude and determination. She would need all of this and more in her lifetime. And one of the greatest tests of her ability to persevere would involve a young man, who, at the time of her youth, was becoming a man.

4

JOHN

WEST POINT

Dinna forget.

The sheer majesty of the United States Military Academy (USMA) surely presented an inspiring yet daunting picture to newly arriving plebes. Set on one of the most remarkable pieces of real estate in the country, the view-shed from its storied halls was then, and is now, stunning. The vistas from high above the western banks of the scenic Hudson River rival the visual splendor of sites familiar to even the most well-traveled souls. But before long, the new arrivals, whether well-traveled or not, found the surrounding scenery to be the last thing on their minds as they came to grips with life as cadets at West Point. John Reynolds was one such individual.[35]

The original Fortress at West Point finds its roots in the Revolutionary War. General George Washington made the newly constructed fortifications his headquarters in 1779. The bastion was never taken by the enemy, and today it remains the nation's oldest continuously occupied military post. By the beginning of the nineteenth century, sentiment was strong for a national military school to ensure domestic expertise in the art of war. The concept had been supported by the likes of Washington, Hamilton and Adams. But as with the Declaration of Independence, it would be left to Jefferson to put pen to paper. Jefferson did just that in 1802 when he signed the legislation that established the U.S. Military Academy on the bluffs of West Point, New York.[36]

West Point, from Fort Putnam, 1859 (B.G. Stone). *West Point Museum Collection, United States Military Academy.*

Despite Jefferson's good intentions, the earliest years of the fledgling school proved difficult, to say the least. In fact, the mere concept of the academy became so controversial that its survival seemed quite uncertain. Indeed, the first several years of its existence seemed to point more to its failure than to its success. Much of this was likely due to the school's startling lack of rules and regulations. Hard to believe as it may seem, in the formative years of the academy there was no standard curriculum and there were no regular textbooks. Moreover, class attendance was optional. And any effort to ensure discipline outside the classroom was exacerbated by the fact that cadets were housed in numerous local boardinghouses. Adding to the overall problem set was the fact that entrance to the academy was gained without either physical or mental examination. The age range for cadets during the academy's earliest years ranged from ten to thirty-four, with some cadets completing their studies in as little as four months while others pushed the envelope at over five years. Given these chaotic circumstances, there is little wonder that support for the school faded quickly over its first decade and a half.[37]

Enter Colonel Sylvanus Thayer. Even in modern times, a superintendent can set the tone for success at any given military academy. Never was that more evident than at West Point in 1817, the year Thayer was appointed

Superintendent Sylvanus Thayer, known widely as the "Father of the Military Academy." Thayer implemented widespread changes in curriculum and discipline that placed the school on solid footing both academically and militarily. His legacy endures to this day (portrait by Robert Weir). *West Point Museum Collection, United States Military Academy.*

superintendent. Destined to become known as the "Father of the Military Academy," Thayer immediately began to implement changes that not only ensured the immediate success of the school but also held it in good stead for decades to come. These modifications were critical, perhaps more so than even Thayer himself imagined, as, unbeknownst to him, these were the decades leading up to the Mexican War and the U.S. Civil War. At the time, the academy had become known as something of an adventuresome escapade for the sons of the rich and famous. Thayer's changes would do much to dispel this notion.[38]

Thayer oversaw key changes that included instituting a firm emphasis on improved academic standards, an insistence on military discipline and an ironclad requirement for honorable conduct among cadets. But the most lasting effect came with Thayer's commitment to establishing the academy's reputation as a center of excellence for training civil engineers. Engineering, science and mathematics would be the foundation on which everything else was to be built. Though Thayer left the academy in 1833, the adjustments and modifications he implemented had taken root by the time John Reynolds arrived. And these changes served to shape John Reynolds not only as a cadet but also as an aspiring soldier and leader of men.[39]

Reynolds arrived at West Point in June 1837 at the age of sixteen. Little did he know he had arrived in the midst of what would later be dubbed West Point's "Golden Age." This was the time between Thayer's departure and the onset of the Civil War. At West Point, Reynolds found himself almost 200 miles from his birthplace. Coincidentally, he was also less than 200 miles from the birthplace of Kate Hewitt. At the time, she had just seen her first birthday, and it would be twenty-three years before they met. Interestingly, when this fateful encounter eventually took place, it would occur some 2,900 miles from West Point. Yet in a sense, Reynolds's journey toward her began at West Point.

Regarding Reynolds's four years at West Point, we are fortunate in that the letters he wrote to his family highlight a number of his experiences. The first encounter he described to his family involved his time tenting on the "Plain." More accurately, this was Sylvanus Thayer's recently introduced "summer encampment," an exercise designed to ready plebe candidates for the rigors of life as cadets and ultimately as soldiers. In his first letter "home," which was actually written to his brother William (officer in the U.S. Navy) during the late summer of 1837, Reynolds expressed his ambivalence with all things West Point, "I begin to tire of living in Camp and wish we were in Barracks. I am very much pleased with my life here and think I shall continue

Summer encampment, 1857. John Reynolds's experience would have been much the same during the summer of 1837. *Class Album Collection, Special Collections, United States Military Academy.*

to like it." Reynolds's biographer Edward Nichols saw this sentiment as an indication of Reynolds's penchant for restlessness seen often in his letters home throughout his ensuing career with the army.[40]

In the same letter, Reynolds also hinted at a bit of homesickness. But that much was to be expected. Soon enough, his studies and his duties served to make him feel more like he belonged. As the saying goes, "misery loves company," and there was plenty of misery to go around. As he subsequently conveyed to his sister Lydia, the rigorous schedule of a fourth classman (freshman) occupied nearly every minute of his day, "From 5 o'clock in the morning, or speaking 'a la militare' from Reveille, until 10 o'clock at night we have only two hours to ourselves." And according to Reynolds, cadets could not "even visit our neighbours [*sic*] without getting 5 demerits."[41]

Regarding Reynolds's companions in "misery," it appears that sharing common experiences did indeed help him form bonds with his fellow classmen. Anything but gregarious, the plain-speaking and hardworking Reynolds endeared himself to his peers and professors alike and even became known as "Josh" to his classmates. Ultimately, the "green" plebe, who in his first letter home had expressed disinterest in the annual cadet ball, did a complete 180-degree turnaround as he raved about his experiences attending the annual ball and other social events as a first classman (senior).[42]

Fellow cadets he encountered during his tenure at West Point ran the gamut from those destined for greatness to those fated to a life of anonymity and everything in between. One of Reynolds's friends with whom he would build a lasting bond was a cadet who would find fame during the Civil War—William Tecumseh "Cump" Sherman. Cump Sherman graduated a year prior to Reynolds. Another of his close friends, Joseph Irons, was killed in the Mexican War. And sadly, Reynolds and a number of his classmates were destined to die in the Civil War. In fact, one of his classmates, Richard Garnett, also died at Gettysburg. Garnett did so fighting for the Confederate army.[43]

As far as his professors and administrators, Reynolds mentioned a few that he was not fond of. But most importantly he developed an admiration for, and friendship with, assistant professor Henry L. Kendrick, who taught chemistry, mineralogy and geology. The feeling was apparently mutual. Kendrick highlighted some of Reynolds's most endearing qualities as a cadet as follows:

> *Independent in thought and action, of clear and definite perceptions, his opinions, on all subjects within the range of a young man's discussion, were well formed and well maintained, and yet so calmly and courteously as to leave no sting in the breast of an opponent, but rather higher respect and greater friendship.*

As we shall see, these traits gained the notice of others throughout John Reynolds's military career. Meanwhile, Reynolds was not alone in his fondness for the good professor, who was also known widely by cadets as "Dad" or "Old Hanks." In fact, Kendrick became quite well known as a cadet favorite not only during Reynolds's time at the Point but also for many years beyond. Cadets appreciated the wisdom Kendrick imparted to them as well as his congenial manner and less-than-pious ways unlike those of many other instructors. But there was more. Some of the cadets' fondest memories of Kendrick involved his kindness in hosting informal Saturday afternoon get-togethers, where servings of brandy-laden peaches and scrumptious waffles (replete with maple syrup) were the primary fare. In later years, it seems that accepting a dish of the delectable mix somehow circumvented a cadet's pledge to the commandant to forgo imbibing in alcohol.[44]

Reynolds's coursework at the academy varied during his four years to include classes in mathematics, French, rhetoric, drawing, chemistry, natural and experimental philosophy, ethics, mineralogy and geology, engineering

One of John Reynolds's favorite professors and lasting friends was Professor Henry L. Kendrick, better known as "Old Hanks" or "Dad" Kendrick. This image, titled "Officers Mess 1878," shows the much beloved Kendrick (*center, silk top hat*) surrounded by younger faculty and an admiring canine. *Class Album Collection, Special Collections, United States Military Academy.*

(civil and military), science of war, infantry tactics and artillery. Reynolds's letters reveal his disdain for French and math while conveying his fondness for artillery training. Reynolds's favorite course, by far, was horsemanship. As a second classman (junior), he noted not only that riding lessons had begun but also boasted that "by the time I graduate I expect to be a great horseman." Reynolds's boast proved prophetic—as we shall see, stories of his riding prowess became the stuff of legend.[45]

As far as academics, John Reynolds proved to be more or less a middling student throughout his years at West Point. At the end of his second year, he stood thirty-fifth out of sixty-eight and by the time of his graduation in 1841 he stood squarely in the middle of his class, ranked twenty-sixth in a class of fifty-two. Regardless of standing, Reynolds was a West Pointer and a full-fledged member of the so-called Long Gray Line. Reynolds had wrestled with a decision over which branch of the service to follow, either

Academy Buildings, W.P.

This 1840s view of the academy and the plain shows the grounds much as they would have appeared to John Reynolds. *West Point Museum Collection, United States Military Academy.*

the dragoons (mounted infantry, the precursor to cavalry) or artillery. Each involved horses and, therefore, was to his liking. Fittingly, after graduation on July 1, 1841, Reynolds was commissioned brevet second lieutenant in Company E, Third United States Artillery Regiment. Reynolds's apparent fondness for artillery and horses would be put to the test during his career as a soldier, perhaps nowhere more than in Mexico during the war of 1846.[46]

When Reynolds left West Point in the summer of 1841, he did so with a uniquely designed class ring that featured his class motto—"Dinna Forget." The sentiment behind the old Scots phrase was likely that the class members would "never forget" the experiences they shared and the bonds they formed as cadets. In one of his last letters home from West Point, John Reynolds waxed sentimental about the memories he had built at the academy and the deep friendships he had made. The spirit of these bonds would be sorely tested some twenty years later in the American Civil War.

By that time, Reynolds had given his class ring to a young woman named Kate Hewitt as a sign of his love. By then, Kate very likely preferred to do anything but remember the life she left behind in California. Long before all of this though, Reynolds's commitment to the West Point school motto of "Duty, Honor, and Country" would come to the fore in a place he very likely never expected to be in his life—Mexico.[47]

5

JOHN

ARMY LIFE AND THE MEXICAN WAR

This has been the greatest battle yet.

He was proud to be in charge. John Reynolds was fresh out of West Point and, as they say, still wet behind the ears. But in his first military assignment at Baltimore's famed Fort McHenry, Reynolds soon enough found himself, albeit temporarily, in command. Writing to his father in early October 1841, Reynolds said, "I have at length made my way to the end of my journey and am now very comfortably situated in our Drawing Room at Ft. McH. in the capacity of Officer of the Day and in command of the fort." Thus began John Reynolds's love affair with the army.[48]

Life in the army would not always be so easy. In fact, between 1841 and 1861 Reynolds traveled far and wide. In the process, he saw action in the Mexican War of 1846–48, almost came to blows with Mormons in Utah and fought against the Pacific coast Rogue River Indians. Besides experiencing the aforementioned "highlights," he also came to grips with all the tedium, discomfort and loneliness he could stand. But throughout all of it John Reynolds seemed to have found a second home. Certainly, all available accounts indicate he relished a life spent both outdoors and around horses. That is not to say he did not have complaints. Like all soldiers, he griped about various aspects of soldier life, most especially the slow rate of promotion and the lack of prime assignments. But in the end, there was no mistaking the fact that Reynolds was right where he wanted to be—in the army.[49]

The first few years of army duty proved relatively uneventful for Reynolds. As a member of Company E, Third U.S. Artillery, he saw garrison duty in a number of locations along the Atlantic Seaboard. After a relatively short stint at Fort McHenry, Second Lieutenant Reynolds was sent to Florida's St. Augustine. While stationed there during July 1842 he fell seriously ill with what was termed "bilious fever." But he was young and strong, and he soon recovered.[50]

In the spring of 1843, Reynolds and his company received notice of their transfer to Charleston, South Carolina's Fort Moultrie. Unlike St. Augustine, this was prime duty, as it afforded the soldiers many opportunities for social activities such as balls and parties. While there, Reynolds deepened his bonds with some of his comrades in arms such as fellow West Point graduates George H. Thomas and "Cump" Sherman.[51]

While Charleston was proving to be an enjoyable posting, August 1843 brought sad news. Reynolds's mother had died. Making things even worse for Reynolds at the time, he was in temporary command of his company and was unable to attend his mother's funeral. Finally, in March 1845, Reynolds received approval for a twenty-one-day period of leave that ultimately turned into three months. It was good that he and his family could spend some quality time together because storm clouds were brewing in Texas.[52]

By the summer of 1845, Reynolds found himself back on duty, this time in Texas. The U.S. government's interest in annexing Texas had stirred up quite a whirlwind. The situation was especially bad along the disputed border with Mexico. And that is where John Reynolds "saw the elephant" for the first time. As it happened, Braxton Bragg's Third U.S. Artillery, Company E (Reynolds's company) was attached to General Zachery Taylor's army. With this, the young artillerist found himself with a front-row seat to a nation on the precipice of war. Though Taylor's army arrived at Corpus Christi in August 1845, it was not until mid-March of 1846 that Taylor marched his army from Corpus Christi, Texas, to the Rio Grande, having established his base of supplies south of Corpus Christi at Point Isabel.[53]

Upon arriving at the Rio Grande, just across the river from the Mexican village of Matamoros, Taylor established an earthen stronghold he dubbed Fort Texas. The six-sided star-shaped redoubt featured 9-foot-high and 15-foot-wide "walls" that extended from 125 to 150 yards each. A 20-foot-wide and 8-to-15-foot-deep moat encircled the exterior of the fort.[54]

The Mexican forces responded to Taylor's presence and his newly constructed bastion by moving north to cut the U.S. Army off from its base of supplies. Taylor quickly moved with most of his army, some two thousand men, to cut off the Mexican effort to leave his army stranded. But he left a skeleton force at Fort Texas. It was good that he did so because when the Mexican army commander General Mariano Arista failed to beat Taylor to Point Isabel, he detached a force to lay siege to Fort Texas.[55]

Fortunately, the garrison was left in the able hands of Major Jacob Brown, who commanded one regiment of infantry and two companies of artillery, including Reynolds's company. Early on the morning of May 3, the Mexicans began to bombard Fort Texas. The small force of roughly five hundred men was nearly overwhelmed, but soon enough they returned fire and the heated contest continued into the evening. Within a few days, the pace and amount of firing slackened, but the desultory fire still threatened life and limb. In fact, on May 6 Major Brown was hit in the leg by a cannonball, and he succumbed to his wounds on May 9, 1846.[56]

Relief finally arrived as Taylor, fearing for the men left holding the bag at Fort Texas, began to force back the Mexican forces that had attempted to cut him off from his base of supplies. As a result of this movement, the war with Mexico began. Taylor's army summarily defeated Arista's army at Palo Alto on May 8 and routed the Mexicans again at Resaca de la Palma on May 9. As a result of Arista's defeat, the forces besieging Fort Texas were also forced to retreat across the Rio Grande. Casualties at Fort Texas were light, with Major Brown and one other soldier the only two killed in the siege of the fort. General Taylor honored Brown, who had bravely helped maintain troop morale during the siege, by renaming the fort in his honor.[57]

A month later, Reynolds expressed his feelings about his "baptism of fire" in a letter to his sister Jennie: "Of one thing I am certain, I can never again, I don't think, be placed in a more uncomfortable situation than the one we have just got out of. I had rather be on ten battle fields [sic] than take another week's bombardment, such as we had in 'Fort Brown.'" John Reynolds's initial taste of armed conflict was just a prelude for things to come. At least there was some reward for his service, for shortly after this action Reynolds received notification of his promotion to first lieutenant.[58]

It did not take long for Reynolds to see more fighting. However, this time the battlefield was no battlefield at all but rather, a city. By August 1846, General Taylor led a force of approximately six thousand men, half regular army and half volunteer, toward the Mexican city of Monterrey. An army of some seven thousand Mexicans under General Pedro de Ampudia awaited their arrival. In a scenario that sounds more like twenty-first-century fighting in the Middle East, the Battle of Monterrey represented one of the earliest examples of U.S. Army soldiers conducting urban warfare. Zachary Taylor's

Second Lieutenant John Reynolds as he appeared during the early phases of his time in Texas. Reynolds wrote to his sister Jennie in June 1846, after the Fort Texas bombardment, "I was obliged to have my locks curtailed, it was becoming rather too hot for so much covering, so I'll enclose a few locks." To this day, these "locks" reside in the Reynolds Family Papers Collection at Franklin and Marshall College. *Courtesy of Archives and Special Collections, Franklin and Marshall College, Lancaster, Pennsylvania.*

plan called for a multipronged attack. Though the forces to which Reynolds's battery was attached were supposed to simply "demonstrate" (distract the enemy from the primary assault), they were quickly drawn into the action. Coincidentally, the battle opened on John Reynolds's twenty-sixth birthday.[59]

Unfortunately for Reynolds, he commanded a section of horse-drawn artillery that was meant for open battlefield operations, not urban conflict. Maneuvering both the artillery and the horses in narrow city streets proved, at best, difficult and at times downright impossible. Yet time and again Reynolds found a way to train his guns on enemy targets. And though neither the adobe nor the masonry houses proved fruitful targets, his leadership shone brightly throughout. In one moment, he orchestrated the extraction of his two-gun section from a narrow alleyway, an effort that required the assistance of infantry to lift the 880-pound guns (cannon) to turn them completely around. In another episode, while exposed to a "galling fire" amid dead horses and ground "slippery with their gasped foam and blood," the men of his battery stripped the harnesses from the dead horses to refit those that survived. Caught in a vortex of sorts, Reynolds later reported, "I was amidst a continuous shower of grape and musqetry [*sic*], but escaped without a touch. Tho' I had my horse twice hit with a musqet [*sic*] ball. How we all escaped I am unable to imagine, not an officer in the battery was

Third Day of the SIEGE OF MONTEREY. Sept. 23rd 1846.

This image accurately depicts the close-quarters nature of the urban fighting during the Battle of Monterrey. *Library of Congress.*

wounded, but our battery suffered considerable." By December, Reynolds, ever the horseman, was proud to tell his family that his horse "has entirely recovered, and is in much better condition than ever, inasmuch as he can go over his four bars and think nothing of it."[60]

Though most of the artillery actions during the battle proved fruitless, General David Twiggs, who had led the attack in which Reynolds's section of guns was engaged, singled out Bragg's men (including Reynolds) by name. Thus, in his first true battle John Reynolds had not only done well but also was recognized, in writing, in an official report. This was heady stuff for the recently promoted first lieutenant.[61]

By February 1847, circumstances had changed. The Mexican army operated under the direct supervision of the infamous Mexican general Antonio López de Santa Anna. Meanwhile, the lion's share of Taylor's most reliable forces, his U.S. Army regular army troops, had been commandeered by General Winfield Scott (against Taylor's wishes and without his knowledge). With this, Taylor's remaining army of some 4,500 troops (including an estimated 500 regulars) was left quite vulnerable. Fortunately for Taylor, John Reynolds's company of artillery (now under Thomas W.

Sherman) and other artillery units remained with his army. Regardless, this was just the sort of situation Santa Anna relished. Seizing the moment, he moved quickly to strike Taylor's relatively small force with his army of an estimated 20,000 men. The ensuing battle took place at a site known as Buena Vista.[62]

Santa Anna attacked on February 22, the anniversary of George Washington's birthday. After his initial probes, he quickly sought surrender from the U.S. forces. Taylor was not about to surrender without a fight, especially on such a meaningful day. The bulk of the fighting that day took place in the late afternoon, and by day's end Taylor's outnumbered forces had held their ground. Be that as it may, the coming sunrise would bring a fury the likes of which none of Taylor's army, to include Lieutenant John Reynolds, had ever seen.[63]

As David Lavender so astutely observed in his enlightening book *Climax at Buena Vista*, nightfall after the first day's fight brought anything but "firefly weather." At an altitude of six thousand feet the moist mountain air portended a chilly interlude between sunset on the twenty-second and sunrise on the twenty-third. The weather gods did not disappoint. Throughout the night, soldiers were left to contend with bitter cold, wind and a light rain. Already suffering from chills, Reynolds was forced to spend the night sleeping on terra firma. He was concerned that his shivering might suggest an oncoming illness. But he was happy to boast to his sister Jennie that on the morning of the twenty-third, "I never went into action in better spirits in my life, the excitement entirely dissipated any sign of a return of my chills." Apparently, Santa Anna was feeling his oats that morning as well, as the Mexican forces resumed their attack with a vengeance. According to Reynolds, "The morning sun shone on us so brilliantly as to remind one of Napoleon's sun at Austerlitz." And in an account eerily similar to those given some sixteen years later by Union soldiers on the third day of the Battle of Gettysburg, he described the grandeur of the moment just prior to the attack: "I never in my life beheld a more beautiful sight; their gay uniforms, numberless pennants, standards, and colors streaming in the sun shone out in all their 'pride and pomp,' their line appeared about three times as long as ours."[64]

Santa Anna's forces hit Taylor's army in the center and then on its left flank. With the building pressure to defend the line becoming heavier by the moment, the need for effective artillery fire to repulse the attacking forces was acute. After arriving at the front Reynolds's battery bolstered the hard-pressed left. Soon after, he and his men were sent to the north to protect the rear from enemy penetrations. After dropping trail to support one group, his so-called flying artillery again moved to support another group. Arriving as the enemy fled this sector, he was still able to effectively harass their retreat, as described by one eyewitness: "He had brought his section into battery just below the hacienda" and "he continued to play upon them with astonishing accuracy and great execution." Then, during one critical moment, Reynolds's section (two cannons) limbered up yet again and moved to the south, back toward the left of the main line. Setting up there in support of Jefferson Davis's "Mississippi Rifles," Reynolds and his men provided crucial support. By late in the afternoon, it seemed Reynolds and his men had been here, there and everywhere. So far, Taylor's brave and beleaguered forces had held on tooth and nail despite being especially hard-pressed on their left and rear. But Santa Anna had one more plan up his sleeve.[65]

Santa Anna had undeniably come close to success. To him, perhaps one more colossal assault would be the straw that broke the camel's back. Thus, at around 5:00 p.m. Santa Anna launched a twelve-thousand-man all-out blitz against the center of Taylor's line in an attempt to break his line once and for all. General Wool indicated, "This was the hottest as well as the most critical part of the action." Fortunately for the U.S. forces, both the volunteer and regular army forces stood firm. In doing so, they received critical support from all their available artillery. Arriving to aid the valiant artillerists who had been holding the center of the line, Reynolds's section provided invaluable assistance as the battle reached its crescendo. All along the line, American cannon roared in defiance of the enemy, spewing chunks of metal into the troops storming Taylor's line. In the end, the artillery proved to be the difference maker. General Wool likely said it best, "Without our artillery, we could not have maintained our position a single hour." Taylor's army had held on against tremendous odds. As the battle was reaching its end, the skies opened with a brief earth-cleansing rain. When the sky cleared, a rainbow appeared that spanned the scene of terrible carnage. Though ephemeral, the juxtaposition was not likely lost on the combatants. To many, it must have seemed the heavens were saying, "Enough." Meanwhile, much to the relief of Reynolds and his compatriots, Santa Anna's army began to retreat during the night, and the Mexican forces were completely gone by sunrise.[66]

Within a week of the battle, Reynolds wrote to one of his sisters. In summing up his feelings, his words spoke volumes, "This had been the greatest battle yet. I thought that at Monterrey I had been in a pretty tight place but it was

BATTLE OF BUENA VISTA.

This image not only shows troop movements during the Battle of Buena Vista but also conveys the grandeur of the scene and accurately portrays the terrain on which the battle was fought. *Library of Congress.*

nothing to this. For eight hours incessantly we were in the hottest places." After accounting for some of his unit's casualties, he summed up his account of the battle by stating, "We are pretty well used up, both men and horses."[67]

John Reynolds had come a long way, both literally and figuratively, in six years. The neophyte officer who had been so flushed with pride in his first assignment at Fort McHenry had seen a lot. Routine garrison duty had provided its requisite ups and downs, but active campaigning and fighting battles had proven to be an altogether different experience. In looking back, Reynolds knew that the events he experienced in the war had shaped him. Like all soldiers subjected to warfare, he would carry parts of what he saw and heard with him for the rest of his life. Unbeknownst to him, his future fiancée would someday encounter life-altering experiences of her own, but of a completely different nature. Yet those experiences shaped her life in a similar fashion. And ultimately, they did so in a way that would lead her to John.

6

KATE

CALIFORNIA GIRL

The Woodward Conundrum…

Statehood came to California in October 1850, but by that time, it was already known for something else—gold. To be sure, San Francisco and its environs in the 1850s was gold country and served as the epicenter of all things gold. When gold was discovered at California's Sutter's Mill in 1848, those seeking their fortune in gold began to arrive. Meanwhile, the city of San Francisco and its citizenry survived a series of devastating fires between 1849 and 1850. But with each fire, they rebuilt, gradually learning the lessons of using less volatile building materials. It was good that they did, as the passion for gold brought a colossal surge in population. Soon, an entire economy developed around the miners' needs. And ultimately, what had once been a relatively modest trading post became the fastest growing city on the continent.[68]

On one end of the expansion spectrum there were hotels, boardinghouses, banks, newspapers, cafés and even a prominent bookseller. At the other end there were bars, gambling rooms and brothels—often one in the same. In between, there were a plethora of businesses centered on bringing speculators to the scene of the action. San Francisco's transportation industry grew by leaps and bounds, especially shipping, but a cottage industry for carriages, wagons and horses emerged as well. Commercial activities centered on the waterfront, and most everything else revolved around Portsmouth Square. Of course, like any city, there was crime. In San Francisco though, there

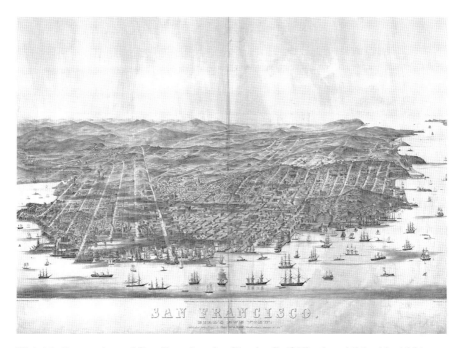

This bird's-eye view of San Francisco by Charles B. Gifford, published in 1864, shows San Francisco much as it would have appeared when Kate Hewitt arrived in the area. *Library of Congress.*

was lots of it. Indeed, the streets of San Francisco were not for the faint of heart. In turn, with crime came law enforcement and jurisprudence. In time, there would also be culture—theater, music and art. But more than anything, San Francisco was its people, people of every conceivable ilk. The influx of citizenry included people from all over the American continent and beyond. There were large numbers of immigrants, especially Chinese. Some of these newly arrived Californians prospered, and some did not. Those who did prosper demonstrated an ability to do whatever it took to succeed, both good and bad. To wit, men were everywhere, and large numbers of the women plied their trade as prostitutes—some likely without choice, others seizing an opportunity. This then was the world Kate Hewitt entered into when she arrived in San Francisco sometime during the mid- to late 1850s.[69]

One popular San Francisco attraction established in 1860s boasted an owner who proved significant in the life of Kate Hewitt and, in turn, John Reynolds. The attraction was the brainchild of one R.B. Woodward. Known as Woodward Gardens, this unusual place of amusement combined the flowers of New York's Central Park with the fauna of a zoo and the

This image shows Kate Hewitt as she likely appeared in the early to mid-1850s. The image, which is part of the Reynolds Family Collection at Franklin and Marshall College, in Lancaster, Pennsylvania, is most likely a copy of an original created at an unknown studio. This presumed copy was created by C.H. Spieler's Philadelphia studio, and the tax stamp on the back side of this image indicates it was likely created sometime between August 1864 and August 1866. *Courtesy of Archives and Special Collections, Franklin and Marshall College, Lancaster, Pennsylvania, caption developed in conjunction with R. Coddington and E. Topping of* Military Images *magazine.*

museum-like aura of the Smithsonian. By the time Woodward opened Woodward Gardens, he was already known for his San Francisco hotel and temperance establishment, the What Cheer House. But despite his role in both enterprises, it was Woodward's earlier possible involvement in the life of Kate Hewitt that might have had the most lasting impact.[70]

Kate Hewitt's foray to California represents yet another mystery in her life. The circumstances around her going there, and the reasons why she did, remain uncertain. According to an article written by Mary R. Maloney during the summer of 1961, Kate was hired in 1856 to travel to the West Coast with the family of one G.R. Woodward. Per Maloney, Kate was to be a governess for two of Woodward's daughters and a son. Though speculation runs the gamut, it is not known for certain whether G.R. Woodward was a friend or family relation. Maloney's article provides the first mention of this scenario, and numerous other secondary sources published after Maloney's article piggybacked on this information, with some embellishing the story. Unfortunately, no primary source for the Woodward scenario in Kate's life is cited in Maloney's article, nor has any been found to date. Yet other information presented in Maloney's article does stem from reliable primary sources, and with this, her research seems sound. Thus, the scenario seems plausible. But the fact that no documentation can be found to indicate a G.R. Woodward lived in San Francisco (or surrounding areas) at the time presents a problem. Unfortunately, no such person shows up in either the relative census reports or city directories.[71]

However, it is interesting to note that the aforementioned R.B. (Robert Blinn) Woodward did live in San Francisco during Kate's time there. R.B. Woodward became a prominent citizen of San Francisco, and—as previously discussed—he owned and operated a well-known hotel. Considering this, we are left to wonder if Woodward's initials (R.B.) could have, for whatever reason (such as a mistake in transcription) been listed differently in Maloney's original source (whatever the source was). For example, could "M.R." (possibly for "Mister") somehow have been mistaken for "G.R." in the transcription? Without the original source, we cannot be certain. However, other available documentation lends itself to the belief that Kate Hewitt did in fact travel to California to work for the family of R.B. Woodward.

First, in 1860, R.B. Woodward's brother William Woodward married a woman named Abby Champlain at Robert's San Francisco home. This is worth noting because Abby was from Owego, New York. Interestingly, though Abby was from Owego, she had also lived, for a short period of time, in Warren, Pennsylvania. (Warren is on the northern border of Pennsylvania, south of Owego, New York.) This is where the plot thickens. Kate's brother Benjamin Hewitt also lived near Warren, Pennsylvania, for a short period of time. And he lived there at the same time as Abby.[72]

Just a few years after living in Warren, Abby returned to and was living in Owego, New York. And sure enough, around the same time, Benjamin Hewitt relocated to Owego. Thus, there appears to be some sort of nexus between Abby and Benjamin. Unfortunately, no documentation can be found to reveal the nature of this nexus. Could there have been some sort of familial connection? And if so, could this possibly be how Kate ended up traveling to San Francisco? Logically, all of this seems to fit and would explain how Kate might have come to work for the Woodward family.[73]

Next, a secondary source, the recently published book *The Two Catherines*, mentions the possibility that the family of R.B. Woodward was the family that hired Kate to be a governess for their family. The basis for this is a Providence, Rhode Island newspaper article that indicates Robert, his wife and their two children *along with a servant*, boarded the SS *Star of the West* in New York, bound for San Francisco, in early September 1857. With this, it seems possible that Kate might have been the servant listed in the newspaper article. The Woodwards likely needed help with the children, and Kate may have filled that role. Regardless of whether or not this was the case, we do know the Woodward family arrived in San Francisco on the steamer SS *Sonora* on October 1, 1857.[74]

In the end, though it is by no means certain, it does seem plausible, and indeed highly likely, that Kate traveled to California to work for one R.B. Woodward (not G.R. Woodward) as a governess for his family. But in the final analysis, whether or not Kate was a governess for R.B. Woodward's family or another Woodward family, numerous primary source documents do show us that Kate was definitely in California in the late 1850s. However, by then she was certainly not working as a caretaker for young children.

7

JOHN

GO WEST YOUNG MAN

Reynolds Luck.

Between 1850 and 1860, John Reynolds's record reflects a period of mostly uneventful experiences, at least compared to his Mexican War service. During this period, he lived the mundane, often lonely and always arduous life of an army officer at sundry duty stations. His years of service during the decade were sprinkled with occasional periods of leave, normally spent at home in Lancaster, Pennsylvania. Having said all of this, it is no small matter that during this same period Reynolds crossed the continent twice, nearly drowned in a perilous voyage and saw action with the Rouge River Indians of the Pacific Northwest. Thus it seems even during relatively uneventful times John Reynolds found adventure.

It was December 1848. The war with Mexico was over, and Reynolds finally traveled home for a period of leave, his first in over three years. The first lieutenant and brevet (honorary rank) major had served admirably with his artillery regiment during the war, and to his family and his neighbors he was a bona fide war hero. The Lancaster community wanted to honor him with a special dinner, but he turned it down. As he was normally reticent, this was not out of character for Reynolds. Yet one must wonder, might he not have been suffering with some degree of battle fatigue or, as it's called today, PTSD? Such analysis is far beyond the scope of this book, but the possibility demands at least a mention. Regardless, it appears Reynolds thoroughly enjoyed this long overdue time with his family.[75]

It is worth noting here that through the entire period of Reynolds's service, family remained extremely important to him. The many letters he wrote to his family, especially his sisters, demonstrate constant concern for his brother in arms, naval officer William. But he reserved his most endearing affection for his sisters. Over the years, the letters he penned to his sisters—Lydia, Kate, Jennie, Hal and Ellie—revealed the emotions of a man to whom family meant everything. Quite often he apologized for not having as much time to write as he would have preferred. As the older girls found their mates, he began to look out for and communicate more with his youngest sisters Hal and Ellie. He showed special interest in his sisters' well-being, both emotional and financial. But there was tenderness in his communications as well. For example, while on duty in Maine one winter, he made sure to profusely thank his fourteen-year-old sister Hal for the handmade scarf she had sent him, even telling her the scarf had made him the envy of everyone at the fort.[76]

Regarding family, or more accurately, Reynolds's wish to one day have a family of his own, one letter stands out. Written prior to his leaving Mexico, in January 1848, John informed his sister Jennie, "I must come to the conclusion—though I struggle against it most heroically, that I am looking old. Yes! Really getting old!" He went on to indicate that he hereby authorized his sisters "to receive proposals for me." Here it seems the confirmed bachelor might not be such by choice. Whether he made this request in jest, or was serious, is unclear. Yet it spoke volumes. John Reynolds, the ever-loving bachelor, was beginning to hear the clock ticking. And he did not want his chance to marry and raise a family to pass him by. Little did he know it then, but he was on the right path. However, it would be a while before fate brought him to the time and place where he might finally find the woman of his dreams. Until then, there was always the army.[77]

By early January 1849, Reynolds was back on duty, this time at Fort Preble, Portland Harbor, Maine. After a few years there, it was off to Newport, Rhode Island, and Fort Adams, and a year later he was transferred to New Orleans.[78]

In May 1853, Reynolds lost his father to a sudden stroke. Once again, he was not home when a parent died (recall he missed his mother's death and funeral). But at least this time he would be able to travel home right away to be with family. John had been extremely close with his father, and he had no stronger advocate. There has been some confusion over whether or not Reynolds was already home when his father died or if he immediately

Two of John Reynolds's sisters, Eleanor (Ellie, *standing*) and Harriet (Hal) Reynolds. Eleanor was largely responsible for preserving the letters sent to her and her sisters by John throughout his military career right up until Gettysburg. *Courtesy of Archives and Special Collections, Franklin and Marshall College, Lancaster, Pennsylvania.*

traveled home. A close analysis of the family letters seems to indicate he traveled home right after learning about his father's death.[79]

Later, while back on duty in New Orleans, Reynolds experienced a bout of yellow fever. Young and strong as ever, he recovered. But recovering from an emotional setback like losing his father was not so easy. A letter written five months after his father's death illustrates John's lasting grief and his deep love of family. His sister Ellie had forwarded him a letter that concerned their father's passing. The letter was written by their brother William and his wife, Becky (nicknamed Be). After reading the poignant note, John responded to Ellie:

> *I read with feelings of brotherly love warming towards them, their deep expression of sympathy with us in the loss of our dear Father. I return you the letter; it is well worthy of their warm hearts and I trust we may all be influenced by the same filial love which we know has been a striking trait in the character of both Will and Be, and I look forward to the pleasure of meeting them and you all once more under the family roof as the greatest time has in store for us.*[80]

For Christmas 1853, John Reynolds's emotions received just the elixir they needed, as he was home on leave. After enjoying the holidays with his family, it was off to yet another duty station, albeit one much closer to home—Fort Lafayette, located in New York Harbor. At this point in his career, Reynolds had not seen any duty on the West Coast. All that changed in the spring of 1854, when he received orders to California.[81]

While Reynolds had been on leave, an estimated 503 members of the Third U.S. Artillery sailed from the Port of New York on December 22, 1853, bound for California (via Cape Horn). The relocation was meant to buttress existing efforts among existing U.S. Army personnel to protect the growing population in California and Oregon from increases in crime (largely spurred by the gold rush) as well as the ever-present threat of hostile Indians. Sailing on the maiden voyage of the pride of the Pacific Mail Steamship Company's fleet, the brand-new SS *San Francisco*, seemed to promise an uneventful trip for the members of the Third U.S. Artillery. Sadly, that was not to be the case. In fact, the voyage proved to be one of the greatest seaborne tragedies of the nineteenth century.

The day after departing New York, the *San Francisco* encountered a growing storm alternately described in contemporary accounts as either a horrific gale or terrible hurricane. We know now it was not a tropical storm but rather a severe extratropical storm, likely a nor'easter. Regardless, some three hundred miles off of the coast of Delaware, the furious storm pounded the *San Francisco* unmercifully for two days. By Christmas Day, the ship had suffered severe damage and lost both its sail and steam propulsion. And sadly, numerous souls had been swept from the ship's main deck by the raging seas. Disabled and severely damaged, the unfortunate ship and all aboard it were left in an extremely perilous situation for several days, with the ship itself left to bob like an unwieldly cork amid storm after storm. Meanwhile, things went from bad to worse as cholera set in among the passengers. Over the course of the ensuing ten days, the survivors were rescued by a series of vessels, but there was much suffering and death before all reached safe haven. Despite the rescue efforts, an estimated 158 members of the Third U.S. Artillery died as a result of the calamity, either by drowning, injuries suffered as a result of storm damage to the ship or cholera. In considering all of this, it appears John Reynolds was quite lucky to have been on leave at the time. Viewed alongside his brushes with death in Mexico, it seems fortune had once again smiled on Reynolds.[82]

Some of the surviving members of the Third U.S. Artillery sailed to California in April on other vessels, but a number of the lot joined Reynolds (Companies A and H) in May 1854 when together, they set out for California, this time via an overland route. In a letter to Ellie, Reynolds mentioned how

THE WRECK OF THE STEAM SHIP "SAN FRANCISCO."

John Reynolds narrowly missed the perilous voyage of the SS *San Francisco*, as the ship sailed with a large portion of the Third U.S. Artillery. *Courtesy National Archives, photo no. 428-N-9000731.*

these men had been on the *San Francisco* and that they "came back totally disorganized and broken up." Thus, Reynolds had his work cut out for him. The trip began uneventfully enough as the men initially traveled via train. Arriving at Fort Leavenworth, Kansas, Reynolds's group fell under command of the expedition commander, "Colonel" Edward Steptoe (brevet lieutenant colonel). The assembled forces soon stepped out on the well-traveled Oregon Trail. The trip was arduous to say the least. Between Leavenworth and Salt Lake City, Utah, a distance of some 1,200 miles, the column dealt with everything under the sun: horses stampeded and came down with distemper, troops fell ill with stomach ailments and cholera, drastic swings in weather led to trekking over nearly impassable trails and marching through miles upon miles of desert nearly proved impossible. But after a challenging crossing of the Rockies and Wasatch Mountains, the careworn group arrived in Salt Lake on August 3, 1854.[83]

The column wintered in Salt Lake. Here, Reynolds's exposure to the Mormon people and their faith proved not to his liking. He saw Brigham Young's followers as clannish and took great umbrage at their leniency with a group of Indians that had played a role in massacring a group of army engineers a year prior. One bit of good news arrived during Reynolds's time in Utah. In March 1855, he was promoted to the regular rank of captain. That aside, John Reynolds bid good riddance to Salt Lake the following May as Major Steptoe's forces renewed their march to California. After another difficult march, the column arrived at Benicia Barracks, near San Francisco, in early July.[84]

Within weeks, Reynolds's company was transferred to Fort Yuma. The first part of the trip was by sea aboard the SS *Republic* to San Diego, but from there it was a 220-mile march inland that ended with 100 miles of desert heat—according to Reynolds, it measured 120 degrees in the shade. Benicia, with its proximity to San Francisco, had been a prime assignment; Yuma was anything but. Situated at the confluence of the Colorado and Gila Rivers, it was surrounded by desert. Commenting on the uncomfortable heat there, John recalled his mentor Dad Kendrick's way of describing the place as "hell with the fires put out." But Reynolds wrote to his sister Ellie, "I agree with him except I think the fires are hardly out yet."[85]

Fortunately for Reynolds, he did not have to endure the broiling surroundings too long, as by late October 1855 he was on the move again. His latest orders placed him in command of Company H, Third Artillery at Fort Orford, Oregon. This time, Reynolds nearly lost his life in relocating. Steamer travel in the mid-nineteenth century could be risky, as evidenced by the aforementioned loss of so many of Reynolds's fellow members of the Third U.S. Artillery in the sinking of the SS *San Francisco*. And sailing across the Columbia River Bar and into the Columbia River was then, and remains today, one of the most dangerous passages in the world. Known far and wide as the "Graveyard of the Pacific," the treacherous waters at the juncture of the river and the Pacific Ocean have caused hundreds of ships' demise and thousands of drownings. The huge waves and unbridled currents in and around the Columbia defy description. Suffice it to say, an 1850s steamer under duress in this scenario could easily sink and take all its passengers down to Davy Jones' Locker with it.[86]

All of this danger may or may not have drawn Reynolds's attention; regardless, he nearly met his demise on the perilous voyage aboard the SS *California*. As it happened, the ship departed San Francisco on November 6. With this, Reynolds and numerous other army officers, including General Wool, settled in for what they hoped would be a short trip to Oregon. The voyage proved uneventful until the ship arrived at the mouth of the Columbia River. In the words of one witness, "A fierce wind had covered the whole bar from shore to shore and for several miles up and down with white foam." Determined to make passage, the river pilot had the captain put on more steam to force a crossing. Soon enough, a boiler flue collapsed, and this caused a fire. The pilot fled the bridge, but the brave captain called on the crew to increase steam in the other boiler. Meanwhile, the crew and passengers, including the army personnel, worked to extinguish the fire. According to Reynolds, "In a few minutes sufficient steam was got up in the other boiler & the fire subdued." In considering the entire experience, John Reynolds did not mince words; to him it was "all most [*sic*] a miracle we did not strike."[87]

Eventually, the beleaguered ship disembarked a few of Reynolds's fellow servicemen in the vicinity of the Puget Sound. Still waiting for his chance to disembark at Fort Orford, Reynolds remained aboard the ship. Returning to the Columbia, the ship soon floundered again. Entering the bar, the ship encountered gale-force winds for nearly three days. As a result, the ship lost power in one engine and was ultimately forced to revert to sail power. Unable to deliver Reynolds and his men to Fort Orford, the ship's crew somehow restored enough power for the ship to steam back to San Francisco. In the end, the twenty-one-day odyssey left Reynolds right where he started. But at least he had survived the ordeal.[88]

After spending the last part of the year on the Board of Examination at Benicia, Reynolds finally made it to his new duty station. It was early

U.S. PACIFIC MAIL SHIP CALIFORNIA.

John Reynolds was aboard the SS *California* when it nearly sank on the treacherous Columbia River Bar during the fall of 1855. This was not his first close brush with death, nor would it be his last. *Courtesy of the National Postal Museum, Smithsonian Institution.*

January 1856 when John wrote to his sister Ellie, "I am as about as far away as one can get—however I prefer it to Yuma. The climate is healthy & pleasant enough in the summer—at present we are in the midst of the rainy season." Reynolds was correct. Even today, Port Orford (located where Fort Orford once stood) remains one of the most westerly towns in the forty-eight contiguous states.[89]

At this point in his career, John Reynolds was familiar with the so-called Indian Wars. And he had encountered Indians in crossing the continent. But he received his first real introduction to Indian fighting while stationed at Fort Orford. Here, Reynolds and his men, serving under Colonel Robert Buchanan, came face to face with the Rouge River Indians of the Pacific coast. As they were notoriously fierce fighters, conflict with the Rouges promised to be very dangerous. Although it appears Reynolds and his fellow soldiers did skirmish a number of times with the Indians during the three-month campaign, most of his actions amounted to more policing than anything else. Yet the duty was not easy. Reynolds informed one of his sisters that the experience had been "very hard, laborious and fatiguing." The most important thing was that the campaign proved successful in rounding up the most troublesome members of the local portion of the tribe; as a result, the dangers to settlers were greatly reduced. A number of citizens expressed their sincere thanks to Reynolds by presenting him with a gold watch as a token of their appreciation.[90]

By December 1856, Reynolds had been transferred back to the East Coast to assume command of Company C of the Third Artillery, which was stationed at Virginia's Fort Monroe (in Hampton, Virginia, adjacent to Norfolk). Being closer to home afforded Reynolds more frequent opportunities to visit with family, both in Norfolk and Lancaster (as well as in between, in Washington and Baltimore). However, the spring of 1858 portended problems with Brigham Young's Mormons in Utah, and with this, Reynolds and his company received orders to join General Albert Sidney Johnston in Salt Lake. General Johnston had already proceeded in that direction when Reynolds's group began their march. Another cross-country trek ensued for Reynolds and his men, but by the time they arrived at Salt Lake the situation had been defused. By then it was late September, and Reynolds's group would have to winter in Utah. The following June, Reynolds and his men resumed their westward march, and some eight hundred miles later, they arrived at Fort Dalles on the Columbia River. From there they boarded a vessel, leapfrogging another ninety miles west to his new duty station, Fort Vancouver, which was located on the Washington and Oregon border.[91]

By the end of 1858, John Reynolds had experienced the best and worst of what army life had to offer. And along the way, he had seen more than one brush with death. During his first year of service, a terrible illness nearly killed him while on duty at St. Augustine. Several years later, he could have easily fallen prey to an enemy musket ball or artillery fire as he served valiantly in the Mexican War. He survived a bout of yellow fever when many around him did not. Fate chose to keep him off an ill-fated voyage out of New York bound for San Francisco. But in an incident that nearly foreshadowed the type of death suffered by future army legend George C. Patton, who died as a result of an automobile accident, Reynolds almost met his demise in a noncombat travel-related accident. This of course was the voyage on the steamer that blew a boiler, caught fire and nearly sank, more than once. Finally, Reynolds might have easily been killed during brushes with the Rouge River Indians. But somehow it seems fortune had smiled on John Reynolds. At one time in his life, George Armstrong Custer had avoided close encounters with death so many times that he brazenly refereed

John Reynolds as he appeared circa 1858–59, while in Utah. Though he was brevet major in the Third U.S. Artillery at the time, he chose to be photographed in civilian attire. *National Portrait Gallery, Smithsonian Institution.*

Battery C, Third U.S. Artillery on parade at Fort Vancouver, photo dated between January and June 1860. A brevet major at the time, John Reynolds is believed to be the soldier mounted on the white horse to the far right in the image. *Courtesy National Archives, photo no. 111-SC-89759.*

to his penchant for surviving as "Custer Luck." But in the end, his luck ran out. Reynolds was certainly aware of how he, like Custer, had been fortunate enough to skirt death on numerous occasions, even once commenting on the subject. But unlike Custer, Reynolds never boasted. Regardless, John's luck, "Reynolds Luck" if you will, would eventually run out too. But before cruel fate caught up with him, he would enjoy perhaps the greatest and happiest moments of his life.

New Year's Eve 1859 marked the coming of a new decade. Unfortunately, once again, trouble was on the horizon—talk of war was in the air. And this time, it was destined to hit much closer to home as this war promised to pit Americans against Americans, brother against brother. In reality, it would be the worst kind of war—civil war. The term itself proved to be the ultimate oxymoron, as this war would be anything but civil.

But before the first shots of the war were fired in anger, John Reynolds's military service would bring him full circle. During the summer of 1860, Reynolds received orders to report to his alma mater as commandant of the Cadet Corps at West Point. These orders proved fateful for many reasons, both professionally and personally, not the least of which involved a chance encounter that awaited him as he boarded the steamer SS *Golden Age* in San Francisco. This ship would carry Reynolds on the first leg in a series of voyages on which he would meet and share time with a lovely young lady. He came to know this woman as Kate Hewitt. Little did he know that Kate Hewitt had recently been known by another name altogether.[92]

8

KATE

REVELATION AND SCANDAL

"Kate Wentworth" traveling as "Miss Hewitt."

With the mystery surrounding Kate Hewitt and the Woodward scenario serving as a backdrop, we now turn to a shocking revelation, one involving no less than an alias and, of all things, prostitution. Here, it is wise to remember that the study of history often takes one to unexpected places. To be certain, when historians set out to examine a given individual's life story, no matter what preconceived notions exist about that person, they must always follow the facts. Having said this, we now unfold the unexpected revelations pertaining to Kate Hewitt's California years.

The key clue to documenting Kate's California years actually relates to the voyage on which she bid farewell to San Francisco. This is the voyage of the SS *Golden Age*, which departed San Francisco on July 21, 1860. Incidentally, this is the same trip that brought Kate together with John Reynolds. In any event, the crucial clue comes to us in the form of one of those true "golden nuggets" of information that historians might never expect to find. In this case, an extremely detailed article about the voyage (likely written by a newspaper editor for Sacramento's *Daily Bee*, who was also on the trip) provides amazing details on the passage. Notably, these details include insights into the lives of some of the most prominent passengers. One of the passengers mentioned was a young woman described as "Kate Wentworth" traveling as "Miss Hewitt." And sure enough, this reference to a "Miss Hewitt" matches the information for the ship's first cabin passengers, which

This unique image provides an aerial view of Sacramento that shows the city as it would have appeared in 1857. The buildings depicted in the border of the view would have been familiar to Kate Hewitt (alias Wentworth) during her time in the city. *A Birds-Eye View of Sacramento "The City of the Plain" by George Holbrook Baker, 1982/x-01/004, Center for Sacramento History.*

also included John Reynolds. This account clearly indicates that "Kate Wentworth" is Catherine "Kate" Mary Hewitt.[93]

Fortunately, the mention of Kate in the aforementioned article, especially her apparent alias and an affair she was involved in, also pointed to additional sources of information describing her California years. These sources confirm the fact that "Kate Wentworth" was in California as of 1859, and a series of newspaper stories from July of the same year describe her as a prostitute living in Sacramento. Thus, it certainly seems that whatever situation originally brought Kate to the San Francisco area, her circumstances were greatly changed by 1859 and that she had relocated to Sacramento. Still other corroborating articles from California's "River City" during the same time frame indicate Kate worked there as a prostitute or "courtesan." In fact, one article describes her as "the mistress of a Sacramento brothel." Revelation indeed![94]

There was a large prostitute population in Sacramento during this period. One study of the 1860 U.S. Census indicates one of every seven women in wards one and two of the city was a prostitute. And according to various newspaper reports and census listings, most prostitutes seemed to have at least one alias. Indications are that the surname most prostitutes used while in the profession, such as "Wentworth" in Kate's case, was the false name. Given the fact that Kate gave the surname Hewitt when she converted to Catholicism (in 1860–61) and when she entered the Daughters of Charity Community (1864), and given the fact that her brother's surname was Hewitt, it seems certain that Hewitt was her true surname and Wentworth was her "professional" name. The 1860 U.S. Census for Sacramento indicates Kate Wentworth (aka Hewitt), age twenty-five, born in New York, lived in Sacramento as the head of a household that consisted of another female, Mary Worcester, age sixteen (born in Arkansas), and a servant, William Pepper. Kate and Mary are both listed with the occupation "Pros." (in other words, prostitute). Further analysis of the 1860 census and various Sacramento city directories indicates Kate, Mary and William lived on Third Street, between L and M Streets. And within one page before and after the census page listing Kate there are ten to fifteen other single women either living alone or in houses together with the same "Pros." occupation.[95]

The *Encyclopedia of Prostitution and Sex Work* notes, "Most prostitutes in the trans-Mississippi West of the second half of the 19th century entered that profession out of necessity." According to an article titled "Red Light Ladies in the American West: Entrepreneurs and Companions," "Women who were without economic means or support from their extended family often turned to prostitution. A few women who were decidedly entrepreneurs saw frontier brothels like hotels and boarding houses as a good business opportunity." As we shall see, this scenario certainly fits with Kate's claim that she had experienced significant misfortune and was also supporting a child (likely adopted). Nevertheless, before Kate left the West Coast, there was more than one matter to consider.[96]

In 1859, Kate Wentworth (Hewitt) became quite well known in Sacramento and San Francisco, but not in the way she likely would have preferred. The summer of 1859 was a summer like so many others in the San Francisco Bay area, hot inland and chilly on the waterfront. The most famous quote on this unusual meteorological phenomenon is normally credited to Mark Twain, "The coldest winter I ever spent was a summer in San Francisco." This adage held as true in 1859 as it has ever

This 1860s view of J Street between Fifth and Sixth appears to have been taken from a balcony. This view gives one a feel for the nature of Sacramento streets and buildings at the time Kate Hewitt (alias Wentworth) lived in the community. *Courtesy of the Special Collections of the Sacramento Public Library.*

since. What was different in 1859 was the torrid scandal that sent virtual shockwaves all the way from the river city to the city by the bay—the so-called Brewton affair.[97]

Interestingly, the aforementioned article about the July 1860 voyage alluded to a "scandal" involving Kate and a well-known individual named Brewton. Multiple articles published in the area during 1859 covered the affair. In these articles, Kate is variously described as either a "lewd woman" or a "courtesan." But what were the circumstances surrounding the alleged scandal, and who was this man named Brewton?[98]

James Goodwin Brewton, also known as "J.G.," was born in Alabama sometime during 1826. The first evidence of James residing in California comes to us via the U.S. Census of 1850. At the time, James's wife, Olive (who was ten years older than James); their children; and his stepchildren lived in the mining town of Mud Springs, El Dorado County, California. One 1859

This ground-level image shows the hardscrabble nature of Sacramento's streets during the mid-nineteenth century. This is J Street between Second and Third Streets, not far from where Kate Hewitt (alias Wentworth) lived. *Courtesy of the Special Collections of the Sacramento Public Library.*

article described Brewton as a man who "always wore a sanctimonious face and attended church regularly and who was a member of the Legislature for Sacramento in 1855." As of February 1860, Brewton worked as a "merchant." Sources also indicate he was a prominent stock dealer and real estate mogul. While numerous articles accounted for James Brewton's professional life and associated interests, one Sacramento newspaper article hinted at a questionable episode in his personal life. The piece detailed his new "Employment and Real Estate" business but adds the tongue-in-cheek comment, "J. G. Brewton & Co. furnishing female help! That's good for those who know the principal's recent exploits in that line." But what in the world did this mean?[99]

Further investigation revealed the answer. In July 1859, multiple area newspapers ran numerous short stories indicating that the community pillar, James Brewton, had scandalously made plans to abandon his wife and leave the state of California with Kate Wentworth. However, despite James's illicit plans, it was not to be. That was apparently because Kate informed Brewton's wife of the nefarious plan in time for her to stop the plot dead in its tracks.[100]

What was the plan? By all available accounts, it appears Brewton and Kate Wentworth (Kate Hewitt) had schemed to run away together. They had planned to surreptitiously make their way to the San Francisco city wharfs, board a ship bound for Panama, cross the isthmus by train and then board a northbound steamer for New York. From there, they would make a fresh start and begin a new life together. Ironically, the ship they were to take, the SS *Golden Age*, was the same ship Kate Hewitt would leave on almost a year to the day later, the voyage on which she met John Reynolds.

Another published article, a much longer gossip column–type of story, seemed to imply that Kate might have been okay with the arrangements until she found out that Brewton had planned to leave his family with no means of support. Still another article referenced a "card" or "personal ad" Kate published in the *Daily Alta* (a personal rebuttal of sorts to the earlier published reports), indicating Brewton had pressed himself on her "with unsolicited attentions, even to the point of persecution." According to Kate's rebuttal article, she had "frustrated his purpose" and "returned him to his family."[101]

Interestingly, Kate's personal ad also detailed at least a portion of her possible motivations for her profession. It seems Kate's work as a prostitute stemmed from an acute need for money. This need was at least in part because she was supporting a ten-year-old adopted "sister" or "daughter" (assumed to be Catherine Dunn, also possibly listed as Mary North on the 1860 passenger list). Another article mentioned that Brewton had bought tickets on a steamer for himself, Kate and a child, all under the names "Mr. and Mrs. Johnson and child." The article listed the child as "Kate's offspring."[102]

Most variations of the story indicate that Kate took hundreds of dollars from Brewton before contacting his wife. The "card," or personal ad, that Kate sent to the *Daily Alta* offered a staunch defense for herself, her actions and her motives. She accused the author of the original story of not telling the truth. Besides the assertion that Brewton's attentions were unsolicited, she also stated that she gave back the $20,000 to Brewton's wife.[103]

One of the other noteworthy things about Kate's article, besides being extremely well written—attesting to the fact that Kate was well educated—is her mention of the fact that she had experienced a life full of misfortunes. Yet in calling attention to her ill fate, she shows a spirit and determination that speaks volumes:

I am accused by an unthinking writer of "loving money better than the heart's affections." I would ask what right has a relentless world given me to heart's affections? and if money is not my best friend? by which I can cast aside forever, the bonds of cruel, slavish life, that, however abhorrent to the heart, requires the face to wear a smile. Again I have a holier purpose in life than my own interest can give—depending upon me is a pure and innocent child—dearer than life; a child not of shame, but of neglect and poverty—such a purpose would seem to sanctify even a desire to obtain money. I do not assume the garb of hypocrisy, as thousands do, to palliate that which is wrong, but I do assert that however unfortunate I may be in my position in society, the purposes of my life and the impulses of my heart, may be no less generous and noble than those of my sex who have been better protected from the cruel wrongs I have been subjected to.[104]*

All of this leaves one to wonder what specific circumstances led a New York–born orphan and would-be San Francisco governess to end up as a courtesan in Sacramento. Whatever the reasons, Clio, the Greek muse of history, maintains her vigil over these secrets.

That said, we do know this much: Kate Hewitt came to San Francisco to escape an orphan's fate. Allegedly, this new beginning offered hope. But by the summer of 1860, Kate's life in California had taken more dramatic twists and turns than she could ever have imagined. And it appears all of this stirred her to, once again, seek a new beginning. The pursuit of this new start in life began that July when she boarded a vessel in San Francisco. Little did she know that despite all the hardships she had endured, the relentless world she lamented did indeed have something in mind for her "heart's affections."

9

JOHN AND KATE

A FATEFUL ENCOUNTER

They met coming from California…

The cannons roared, and the band played. And with that the well-traveled SS *Golden Age* inched away from its berth in San Francisco Harbor. Thus, with this martial send-off for General William S. Harney and his supporting cast of U.S. Army officers, including Brevet Major John F. Reynolds, the voyage began. As the ship gained steam, the winds picked up and the temperature surely dropped; the vessel slowly made its way toward one of the most remarkable geological formations in the world—the Golden Gate. Bestowed with this name by yet another army officer, the famous "Pathfinder," John C. Frémont, this stunning break in the California Coast Range allows for the connection between San Francisco Bay and the Pacific Ocean. The glacial-formed straits that run through its opening can be among the most perilous passages to navigate. Compounding mother nature's juxtaposition of grandeur and danger, the heavy fogs that typify the conditions present on any given passage through the Golden Gate make doing so an adventure in and of itself. This is true not only for a ship's officers and crew but for passengers as well. The chill of the salt-laden air combined with the heave and yaw of the vessel on the rolling seas test the mettle of even the most stout-hearted of sailors. On the other hand, anyone who experiences the breathtaking moment of passing through the famed Golden Gate will never forget the feeling of exhilaration it brings to the soul.[105]

OCEAN STEAMERS.

P. M. STEAMSHIP COMPANY'S

STEAMSHIP

GOLDEN AGE,

J. T. WATKINS.........................COMMANDER,

Will leave Folsom-street Wharf,

Saturday...............July 21, 1860,

At 9 o'clock, A. M., Punctually,

FOR PANAMA.

Passengers will be conveyed from Panama to Aspinwall by the

PANAMA RAILROAD CO.,

And from Aspinwall to New York by the

ATLANTIC AND PACIFIC STEAMSHIP COMPANY.

FORBES & BABCOCK, Agents,

jy18td   Corner Sacramento and Leidesdorff sts.

Left: This newspaper ad announced the upcoming sailing of the SS *Golden Age. From the* San Francisco Daily Herald, *July 20, 1860.*

Below: This 1863 view of the various wharfs along the San Francisco waterfront illustrates the scene much as it would have appeared to John Reynolds and Kate Hewitt as they embarked for their sojourn to New York during the summer of 1860. *San Francisco Maritime National Historical Park (Image Number A12. 1523.).*

This stunning image of the famed "Golden Gate" offers a glimpse of the scene that captured the imaginations of countless individuals as they sailed through its opening to the deep blue Pacific Ocean. Departing on an early morning voyage to an uncertain future, little did John Reynolds and Kate Hewitt know the voyage would bring them together. *Library of Congress.*

One must wonder what this moment felt like to Kate Hewitt. There she was, embarking on a new life, and not for the first time. But this time she was leaving behind a checkered past. Irrespective of the circumstances, a month after the census that first captured her name for historians (albeit under an alias), twenty-four-year-old Kate sailed away from California, forever. It was the morning of July 21, 1860. The aforementioned article from a local newspaper reporter confirmed the fact that "Kate Wentworth," traveling as "C. Hewitt," departed San Francisco aboard the SS *Golden Age* bound for New York (a sojourn of some three to four weeks). Travel at that time was to Panama, then across the isthmus via rail connection and on to a second voyage to New York. As mentioned previously, Kate was not traveling alone. Apparently, a "ward" about ten years old traveled with her. Though the child was not listed on the published passenger list for the first leg of the sojourn on the SS *Golden Age*, a ten-year-old female by the name of "Mary North" does show up just under Kate's name on the passenger list for the second leg of the voyage aboard the SS *North Star*. In all likelihood, this anomaly can be accounted for by Kate's purchase of a second-class ticket for the child, as the passenger list for the SS *Golden Age* only listed those with first-class tickets. No matter, the girl was with Kate on the trip from start to finish. Further, Miss North is almost assuredly one Catherine Mary Dunn, the same young lady Kate Hewitt later enrolled in

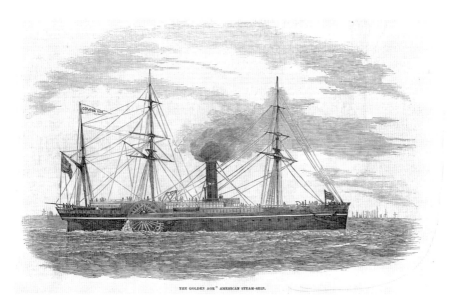

THE GOLDEN AGE" AMERICAN STEAM-SHIP.

The SS *Golden Age* sailed on the morning of July 21, 1860, with some 270 passengers and a valuable cargo estimated at just over $1 million. Numerous individuals of prominence sailed with the ship, including the U.S. Army's General Harney and Brevet Major John Reynolds. Harney's presence drew a splendid send-off, as the First California Guard fired a salute of eleven guns in front of the Oriental Hotel. Also on board, as noted by an astute reporter, was a local woman of note known to most as "Kate Wentworth," who was reported to be sailing as "Miss Hewitt" (*Daily Alta,* July 21, 22, 1860). *From the* Illustrated London News, *October 22, 1853 (via Australian National Maritime Museum website — collections.anmm.gov. au/en/objects/40030/the-golden-age-american-steamship;jsessionid=F5AD4D66FC80CE).*

Eden Hall (Catholic school/convent, Torresdale, Pennsylvania), when she also enrolled herself.[106]

Interestingly, there was no "ward" or child listed with Kate in the 1860 census in Sacramento. It's possible that Kate had put her in a school in the area, but this is only speculation. Regardless, three months after arriving in New York, when Kate applied to attend Eden Hall's Academy of Sacred Heart, she also enrolled her "adopted sister," Catherine Dunn. According to the school's records, Dunn was born on June 28, 1850, in New Jersey. Though it is not certain that Catherine Dunn and Mary North were the same person, it does seem highly likely.[107]

Meanwhile, as detailed in chapter 8, the newspaper account of the trip provides intriguing information related to Kate. As described by the author of the newspaper article:

This extremely rare image of Kate Hewitt, believed to be published here for the first time, appears to show her as she likely appeared in the late 1850s. It was created by C.H. Spieler's Philadelphia, Pennsylvania studio and may very well be a copy of an original created on an earlier date at a different studio. *Courtesy of Katie Cleaver.*

> *Among us were few notabilities, two of whom I will mention—General Harney, and Kate Wentworth, who travels by the name of Miss Hewitt. She was accompanied by her ward, aged about ten years, and an* inamorata *from the vicinity of Nevada. She, who made herself so notorious in the Brewton affair, conducted herself, so far as I know, in a very creditable manner during the trip.*[108]

The article was written and published in September 1860, after the voyage had ended. With this, it is possible that the love interest, or *inamorata*, was in fact John Reynolds. The reference to "Nevada" likely refers to Nevada, California. As discussed, Reynolds was traveling with the highly regarded and well-known General Harney and a few other U.S. Army officers as well. The group was returning to the East Coast on the same series of voyages. It is interesting to note how the author commented on Kate having conducted herself "in a very creditable manner." The article also provides wonderful insight into conditions on the trip. Apparently, the meals on the SS *Golden Age* were anything but satisfying. But per the article, the ship was clean and sleeping conditions satisfactory.[109]

When the first leg of the journey to the East Coast ended in Panama, passengers traveling to New York crossed the isthmus by train to Colon (Aspinwall), Panama. They then boarded the SS *North Star*. The symbolism inherent in the ship's name as a beacon of inspiration and hope likely inspired

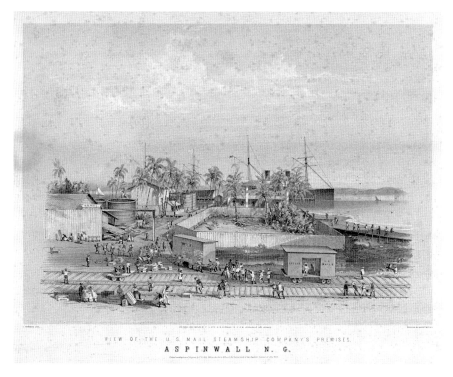

In 1860, passengers traveling from California to New York City by steamship first sailed to Panama, where they were conveyed across the isthmus via a rail line operated by the Panama Railroad Company to Aspinwall (Colon). From there, passage to New York was aboard a vessel of the Atlantic and Pacific Steamship Company. The entire sojourn typically took three to four weeks. *Library of Congress.*

VANDERBILT'S AMERICAN STEAMER, THE NORTH STAR.   [See page 251.]

The final leg of John and Kate's voyage to New York brought them on board the SS *North Star*. According to one chronicler, while the SS *Golden Age* had proven "well manned and kept very clean," the SS *North Star* was "the dirtiest ship I have ever seen." Apparently, the ravaging fleas and bedbugs, as well as the "decks covered with tobacco juice and dirt," had everyone aboard wishing for a quick end to the trip. (Quote from the *Sacramento Bee*, September 15, 1860). *Courtesy of Wikimedia Commons.*

many travelers over the years, perhaps none more than Kate Hewitt. As she sailed toward a new beginning and a fresh start, one would think the irony was not lost on her. That aside, there were the more practical matters of the voyage to consider. The *North Star*'s transit apparently proved uneventful save for the daily need to squash ravening bedbugs. Yet the aforementioned article does indicate that the dining experience on the *North Star* far exceeded that provided on the *Golden Age*.[110]

Despite the less-than-ideal accommodations, the ship arrived safely in New York on August 13, 1860. And sure enough, the passenger list of arriving passengers listed "Miss C. Hewitt," age twenty-three (her age would actually have been twenty-four), traveling in a first (class) cabin. The passenger list also included one "Maj. Reynolds," age forty, U.S. Army.[111]

The journey from San Francisco to Panama to New York City represents a central part of the story of Kate Hewitt and John Reynolds. Undeniably, according to what Kate later told his sisters, this is when she met John Reynolds for the first time. Some previously published secondary source accounts of the saga of John and Kate indicate they met before this voyage. But no known primary source documentation supports this contention. In short, it does not seem likely that Kate knew John prior to boarding the SS *Golden Age* the evening before its departure from San Francisco. John Reynolds was probably not in the San Francisco area for too much time prior to boarding the ship on July 20, 1860. At least one press report indicates that he arrived in the city, along with General Harney, on July 18, 1860. Meanwhile, Kate probably didn't have to be in San Francisco long before the ship departed, as Sacramento was a short boat trip away from San Francisco.[112]

Be that as it may, one is certainly left to wonder exactly how Kate and John met. Surely a novelist could conjure up any number of romantic scenarios. Did their eyes meet with a quick glance at each other while boarding? Or did nineteenth-century chivalry play a role? Perhaps the strikingly handsome soldier in his impressive uniform, replete with shimmering buttons, came to the aid of Kate and Mary as they struggled to maintain their footing on the moisture-laden decks of the vessel while it plunged through the rolling swells of the Pacific Ocean. Possibly the moment was more sublime; a chance meeting while dining, or maybe it was pure happenstance as each sought to gain a position along the ship's rails to gaze on the fading hills of San Francisco as the ship made headway for the Pacific Ocean. Sadly, we will never know. Then again, perhaps some things are best left to the imagination.

Regardless, we know this much: John Reynolds and Kate Hewitt met and fell in love coming from California to New York. Certainly, it was on this voyage that they began to develop a deep affection for one another. Despite the arduous nature of the voyage, the trip afforded John and Kate more than ample time to get to know each other. And it appears the more they learned about each other, the more they were drawn together. Most importantly, the affection resulting from their time together on the SS *Golden Age*, the cross-isthmus train and the SS *North Star* continued to flourish long after their arrival in New York on August 13, 1860.

10

JOHN AND KATE

ENGAGEMENT AND A LAST PROMISE

Her letters were sealed with his class ring…

When Major John Reynolds and Kate Hewitt arrived in New York during mid-August 1860, they did so on the cusp of a tumultuous time in U.S. history. The fratricidal nature of politics and a nation on the brink of war would ultimately affect the future of their relationship in the most tragic way possible. But in August 1860, with their love blossoming, it must have seemed to John and Kate that life had just begun. Yet as their deepening relationship evolved, it relied heavily on written correspondence rather than personal visits, as his responsibility to his life as a soldier severely limited any opportunity for them to keep company. Still, the exact time of their engagement, all these years later, remains uncertain. However, on the occasion of Reynolds's death, Kate provided his sisters with some details pertaining to her engagement to John. In turn, Reynolds's sisters repeated those details in letters they wrote to their brother, naval officer Commander William Reynolds. A close analysis of these letters provides some clues but not all the answers. What follows is an account of what is known and what is not known regarding the engagement of John Reynolds and Kate Hewitt.

Upon arriving in New York on August 13, John Reynolds had a brief opportunity to enjoy Kate's company a bit longer, as he was not due at West Point until early September. However, no documentation exists to confirm his whereabouts during this time. In a notice that appeared in the *New York Herald*, titled "Officers Ordered to West Point," Reynolds is listed as reporting on September 1, 1860, to the Tactical Department at West Point. The West Point "Post Return" for September 1860, the most reliable source, shows his "time of joining" as September 8, 1860. Later, in a letter dated September 20 that he wrote to his sister Ellie, John states, "I have now been on duty here for a week."[113]

It seems likely that Reynolds would have taken advantage of the time available to him between August 13 and September 8, 1860, to visit his family in Philadelphia. And though no evidence survives to indicate he did so, it is well known that he was close with his sisters and thus it certainly seems likely that he visited them while on leave. It is also logical to consider that he may have also spent as much time with Kate as possible during this time. But if he did so, he did so without anyone else's knowledge.

Regardless, the best available evidence available indicates Reynolds gave his West Point class ring to Kate sometime between August 1860 and July 1861, the time of Kate's departure from Eden Hall. And though Kate later informed Reynolds's family that she and John had been engaged, no primary sources exist to confirm that the engagement actually occurred when John gave Kate his ring. That said, it is certainly logical to presume that John asked for Kate's hand in marriage when he placed his ring on her finger, but again, this is not certain.[114]

We do know, per John's sister Jennie, that two letters from Eden Hall signed "Kate" were found in John's valise after his death, and each letter bore the wax seal of John's West Point ring. Sadly, these letters appear to have either been lost or destroyed. This is too bad, because the date of these letters might have offered valuable insights with regard to the date of John's and Kate's engagement. Nor do any letters from John to Kate seem to have survived. Even the letters sent by Kate to John's sisters after his death are missing. In fact, the only surviving documentation relating to John and Kate's relationship and engagement are the letters written by John's sisters Ellie and Jennie, to their brother William, on the occasion of John's death.[115]

This artist's impression, created by Dale Gallon expressly for this book, is believed to be the first-ever accurate representation of John Reynolds's West Point class ring. This is also believed to be the first time ever an accurate likeness of Reynolds's actual ring has been published. *Artist's impression by Dale Gallon, author's collection.*

But here is the important thing to note: the aforementioned letters to John listed Eden Hall in Torresdale, Pennsylvania, as the location of the writer, and each letter bore a waxed seal with the image of John's West Point class ring. This information points to the fact that the letters were sent *after* John gave his ring to Kate. This also means that Kate, in all likelihood, sent the letters while she was living at Eden Hall (November 1860–July 1861). In turn, if the engagement took place simultaneously with John giving Kate his ring, it appears they were engaged some time before the end of July 1861.[116]

Logic would also seem to dictate that John either gave Kate his ring prior to her entering Eden Hall or during some period of leave from his duties at West Point. With John and Kate going their separate ways in September 1860, John might have felt compelled to seek a commitment from Kate before they parted. Certainly, once he assumed his duties at West Point, Reynolds found his leave was quite limited. Yet in a letter written in early December, he makes mention of being in New York City "the other day." Apparently, at least part of this visit was spent with his brother William and his wife, Rebecca. Perhaps John also took advantage of this opportunity to steal a visit with Kate as well. In the same letter though, he indicates, "I am very sorry to say that I shall have to disappoint you all at Christmas, but the Superintendent will not let any of the officers on duty with cadets to leave during the holidays." Thus, it appears there was not only no opportunity for Reynolds to visit with family at Christmas but none to visit with Kate either.[117]

Aside from matters relating to the timing of John's and Kate's engagement, there were physical items related to their betrothal to consider. Here, Reynolds's sisters mentioned how a small gold ring inscribed with the words "dear Kate" was found among his remains. Kate had given this ring to John. What is not known is when she gifted the ring to John and whether or not this was a ring Kate had already owned or if it was one she had made expressly for him.[118]

One clue seems to point to Kate previously owning this ring. One of Reynolds's staff members mentioned the ring being found on John's "little finger" at the time of his death. Certainly, if the ring had been Kate's, it likely would not have fit any of John's other digits. Conversely, if Kate had special ordered a ring for John, one would think she would have had it sized to fit his ring finger, especially if she sought to "replace" his West Point ring. Further, there is the question of when she gave this ring to John. Again, nothing is certain though it seems probable that she did so when he gave her his West Point ring. We also know, per John's sisters' letters, that

Renowned artist Dale Gallon's *Last Promise*, released to great acclaim in 1997, depicts one interpretation of John Reynolds and Kate Hewitt at the moment of their engagement. Last Promise, *by Dale Gallon (www.gallon.com).*

Kate gave John two Catholic items—"a heart and a cross." Both of these items were found on Reynolds's remains, strung on a silken string that hung from his neck.[119]

And finally, as Reynolds's family also learned, Kate made one last promise to John. She likely made this promise when they became engaged, but we have no way of confirming the timing of the promise. Regardless of timing, per the aforementioned letters written by Reynolds's sisters, we do know that Kate Hewitt promised John that she would enter into a religious life if he were to be killed during the war. Sadly, this promise, this poignant and heartfelt commitment, came calling all too soon at a place called Gettysburg.[120]

There was one more thing. John and Kate kept their engagement a secret. No one knows why. The supposition has always been the reason for secrecy centered on their religious differences, as he was Protestant and she was Catholic (after her conversion) and of Irish descent. This may have very well been true, as religious difference issues remained at the fore in mid-nineteenth-century America. But there is no proof of this being the reason. There is also Kate's background to consider. Perhaps John wanted to wait until Kate's conversion was complete, but then war intervened. Whatever the reason, Kate and John's love for each other remained a secret until his death.

In short, it certainly appears as though John Reynolds may have asked for Kate Hewitt's hand in marriage sometime prior to the nation splitting apart. And this engagement likely came on the occasion of an exchange of treasured rings, precious religious items and a deeply meaningful promise. If so, one can envision the occasion of their engagement. Indeed, such circumstances are as old as time. The brave soldier, possibly going off to war all too soon, proposes to the girl he loves. The lovely maiden accepts the poignant proposal while simultaneously feeling the jubilation of engagement and the pangs of fear surrounding an uncertain future. And all of it was a secret.

11

JOHN

RETURN TO THE POINT

I will try for a week or so longer the duties which I find very disagreeable to me…

It must have been a trying time for John Reynolds. The nation was on the cusp of war. He was career army and would certainly be part and parcel to the conflict. As a loving brother to his siblings, he maintained a keen interest in their welfare. And then there was Kate. Finally, he had found the love of his life. But their plans for a life together were on hold due to all the uncertainty and unrest in the nation. All too soon this situation would resolve itself. But before then, Reynolds would experience many twists and turns in his life as a soldier. As commandant at West Point, John Reynolds wore several hats. In the beginning, the assignment was definitely not to his liking. But over the course of his one year in the position, his distaste for his new job would be completely overshadowed by a much greater concern.

The September 1860 "Post Return" for West Point listed Captain and Brevet Major John F. Reynolds with the duties of instructor of infantry tactics, artillery and cavalry. As commandant, Reynolds would also shoulder the responsibility of teaching veterinary science and art, outpost duty, strategy, grand tactics, army organization and administration. And it was no small matter that he also commanded corps formations, parades and more, while also serving as chief disciplinary officer. Though he had a number of assistants, his was undeniably an enormous task. Reynolds was not happy with his new position. Less than two weeks after assuming his position as commandant he expressed his dissatisfaction with the position in a letter he

West Point commandant Major John F. Reynolds. This photo, taken some time between September 1860 and early 1861, shows Reynolds holding his Hardee hat, which was adorned with the crossed artillery tubes marked with the number three, denoting his concurrent status as a member of the Third U.S. Artillery. *Courtesy of Archives and Special Collections, Franklin and Marshall College, Lancaster, Pennsylvania.*

wrote to his sister Ellie: "I will try for a week or so longer the duties which I find very disagreeable to me, so different from anything I have ever had before, & so confining annoying & various, that I have hardly yet had time to test them fully….It is a most exacting one to the patience, industry & temper of any person, & of course very different from commanding men."[121]

Adding to all of this, ensuring cadet discipline with emotions high as the nation crept closer and closer to war represented a greater than ever challenge. In November 1860, Reynolds expressed related concerns to his brother Jim: "We are in the midst of troubles everywhere now & in the present unsettled state of the country we may well ask what is to become of us as well. Even here we feel the effects of this sad condition of affairs, however I hope there will be found a way out [of] all the difficulties, & by a moderate course on the part of both north & south, these old feuds be banished forever."[122]

President Lincoln's election in November 1860 seemed to seal the nation's fate. Soon a number of southern states began to secede from the Union. If there was any doubt as the winter of 1860–61 turned to spring, the firing on Fort Sumter in Charleston Harbor on April 12, 1861, served as the point of no return. In a letter written soon after, John indicated to his sister Ellie, "Here in our quiet nook, we can hardly realize that this great nation is in

This 1869 image, titled "Houses on the Plain," shows the commandant's quarters on the far right. The quarters appears as it would have in 1860–61. *Class Album Collection, Special Collections, United States Military Academy.*

the agonies of dissolution. Tho' we are now beginning to feel it, in a week more & I suppose we will have no southern cadets at the academy." He was not too far off. At the time, there were 278 cadets at the academy, 86 of whom were from southern states. Some 65 of this number either left or were discharged in connection with the war (6 departed for other reasons). But 15 of the southerners remained. Meanwhile, it is also interesting to note that in the same letter (April 25), Reynolds indicates he "was very sad not to have seen you when in Phila." This seems to indicate he had made a trip to Philadelphia around that time. If so, he may have taken advantage of the opportunity to visit Kate. In turn, this represents yet another possible opportunity for the occurrence of their engagement.[123]

Ironically, the cadet who likely caused Reynolds the most heartburn at this time of tenuous political issues was known more for his nonpolitical antics than anything to do with the spiking tensions in the country. This troublemaker was none other than George Armstrong Custer. Last in his class and nearly booted out of the academy due to an extremely high demerit count, Custer was placed under arrest by Reynolds just prior to commissioning for "neglect of duty" (failing to break up a fight between two cadets). Forced to observe commissioning ceremonies from his quarters as he awaited a court-martial, Custer watched his classmates march away from West Point in June 1861. Much chagrined, Custer realized his classmates were headed for Washington, D.C., and service in the war. But Custer's

Cadet George Armstrong Custer graduated last in his class and was under arrest, per orders from Commandant Reynolds, at the time of graduation. *Class Album Collection, Special Collections, United States Military Academy.*

disappointment did not last long, as fate and friends with influence soon intervened on his behalf and he soon joined his brothers in arms.[124]

Perhaps mercifully for Reynolds, his tenure at West Point proved relatively short due to the onset of the Civil War. By July, the war had precipitated John's promotion to lieutenant colonel in the regular army and command of the recently reactivated Fourteenth United States Infantry at Fort Trumbull, Connecticut. The promotion was actually dated May 14, but Reynolds did not receive official notice of his increase in rank and new assignment until early July 1861. By July 3, he was off to the next chapter in his military career and his life. Beyond this, there remained John's relationship with Kate. Certainly, he must have wondered how the war would affect their relationship and their commitment to each other. Only time would tell.

12

KATE

SALVATION AND REDEMPTION

She was endowed with an honorable heart…

K ate Hewitt would once again start anew. For an orphan girl from a
small town in New York to venture out into the so-called cruel world
could not have been easy. Yet somehow Kate Hewitt appeared to
embody all the spirit necessary to not only survive but also thrive in a world
full of less than scrupulous characters. In point of fact, she did just that in
California. Still, it seems something was missing in her life. And whatever
that something was, Kate realized she needed to change her circumstances
to find it. Her soul-searching for what that "something" was must have been
quite deep, for it appears that her answer was religion. Ultimately, she decided
to leave behind her previous life, both physically and figuratively, by turning
to God. In doing so, she was neither the first person to cast aside a sordid
past in order to seek redemption, nor would she be the last. Regardless, the
fact that she did so was a testament to her fortitude, her belief in herself and
her willingness to seek forgiveness for the mistakes she had made. In short,
when Kate Hewitt enrolled at Eden Hall, she aimed to cleanse her soul.

These are the facts. Kate Hewitt and her ward, Catherine Dunn,
both entered Eden Hall Academy of the Sacred Heart on November 10,
1860. While there, they both converted to Catholicism. Kate Hewitt was
baptized into the Catholic faith on March 18, 1861, and she made her
First Communion the next day. Catherine Dunn was baptized on April 30,
1861, and Kate Hewitt was listed as her godmother. Dunn made her First

Eden Hall — yesterday

Kate Hewitt converted to Catholicism at Eden Hall, which was located in Torresdale, Pennsylvania, only a few miles from John Reynolds's sister's home in Philadelphia. *Provincial Archives, Society of the Sacred Heart, United States-Canada Province, Saint Louis, Missouri.*

Communion on May 1, 1861. And they both made their Confirmation on July 5, 1861. Kate Hewitt is listed as leaving Eden Hall immediately after her conversion was complete.[125]

But beyond the simple facts, there was more. It seems Kate Hewitt's way of doing things, her personality if you will, was quite endearing. At Eden Hall, neither her ability to touch hearts nor her proclivity to feistiness went unnoticed. The "Annual Letter" of the Sacred Heart of Jesus Society, the school's yearly report, revealed the details. In the letter, Kate Hewitt's conversion is described as "remarkable." The letter details how, even though she had no real knowledge of the Catholic faith, she was "endowed with an honorable heart, and an energy which renders her capable of overcoming all difficulties, serving without forgetting who the source of light and faith is." The letter continues, "Never has she forgotten self-control, finding within herself the reflection of that light. She has a natural character of a strong impetuous nature, but the religion has helped her to conquer it." Apparently,

This image depicts the Eden Hall chapel as it would have appeared at the time Kate Hewitt attended the school. *Provincial Archives, Society of the Sacred Heart, United States-Canada Province, Saint Louis, Missouri.*

the personality traits that had held her in good stead throughout her life continued to serve her well at Eden Hall.[126]

Beyond the emotional aspects of her conversion, her experiences at Eden Hall provide a glimpse into her interests in the arts and language. In turn, all of this reveals the degree of her financial stability. In the short time that Kate Hewitt was at Eden Hall, she took classes in music, voice, drawing and Spanish while also paying a fee for the use of a piano. She also paid for a uniform and a veil. There were also charges for medical visits and medicines. In all, Kate paid $426 for the period of time from November 1860 to July 1861. In today's dollars, that would amount to a little over $12,700.[127]

After completing her conversion, Kate Hewitt left Eden Hall. Although Catherine Dunn had also completed her conversion, she was still of school age. As a result, Dunn remained at Eden Hall for at least six more years. The exact date for Catherine Dunn's exit from Eden Hall remains uncertain. However, based on the financial records, it appears she was there until February 1866. By then, Kate Hewitt had been a member of the Daughters of Charity community for nearly two years (Kate's experiences with the Daughters of Charity will be detailed in a later chapter).[128]

Aside from the religious aspects of Kate's time at Eden Hall, the aforementioned matter of money presents a few questions. As indicated, attending Eden Hall was an expensive endeavor. Thus, questions remain regarding how Kate might have afforded the school. There are also questions about the funding for Catherine Dunn's time at the school. Later correspondence between John Reynolds's siblings implies that Kate may have been from a prominent family. This seems to conflict with the evidence that she was an orphan. Also, there is the notion that she was allegedly hired as a governess and the fact that her brother was working as a farmhand in the 1850s. All of this seems to lend itself to the impression that, as orphans, Kate and Benjamin were not left a great deal of money from their parents. However, this could be explained if they had not been entitled to whatever estate their parents might have left them until adulthood. Regardless, it appears Kate Hewitt, working as "Kate Wentworth," may have done well for herself financially as a prostitute in California. This alone likely resulted in Kate's financial stability at the time.[129]

Meanwhile, with her conversion to Catholicism complete, Kate could now focus on her newfound love. But the object of her affection, John Reynolds, would find his desire to respond in kind complicated by an age-old factor that destroyed countless courtships—war.

13

JOHN

CIVIL WAR—THROUGH THE RANKS

Now boys, give them the steel, charge bayonets, double quick!

Enough information exists to warrant an entire book on John Reynolds's Civil War years. A thorough analysis of this period of John's life is well beyond the scope and intent of this book. However, John's service in the Civil War is certainly relevant to his relationship with Kate Hewitt. From the time he left his position as commandant of West Point to the beginning of the Gettysburg Campaign, Reynolds made quite a name for himself. Kate Hewitt must have earnestly awaited word from him during this time. Surely, he wrote to her. And certainly, she must have followed the newspapers to glean what information she could about Reynolds's activities, hoping against hope that his name would never appear in the list of casualties. John may have visited Kate during the war, but there is no firm evidence to indicate he did so. Yet he did have a number of opportunities. What follows is a summary of some of the most noteworthy episodes from the war in which Reynolds played a key role. These are episodes Kate may have been aware of through letters from John (similar to those he sent his family), from press reports and perhaps, on rare occasions, from stolen moments with him.

Upon leaving his position at West Point to assume command of the Fourteenth U.S. Infantry, Reynolds found himself in a position more to his liking. Though his preference was for an artillery command, almost anything was better than his West Point gig. However, as soon as he began to settle into his new job he received news of his appointment and promotion to the

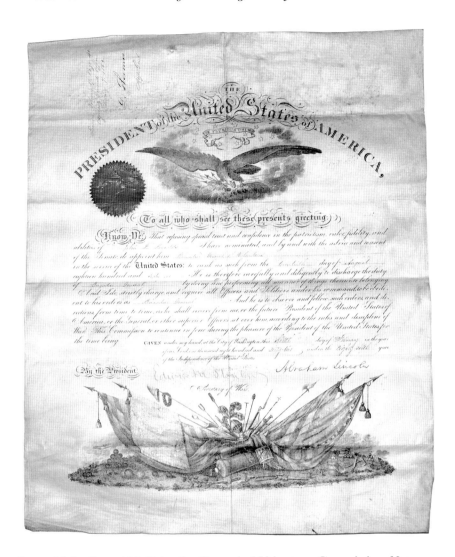

General John Reynolds's Brigadier General of Volunteers Commission. Note President Abraham Lincoln's full signature at the bottom. *Courtesy of The Horse Soldier, Gettysburg, Pennsylvania.*

rank of brigadier general of volunteers, and ultimately this resulted in his transfer to the Army of the Potomac.[130]

Reynolds's journey to his new assignment with the Army of the Potomac, located in the vicinity of Washington, D.C., began when he departed from Fort Trumbull, Connecticut, on Sunday, September 8, 1861. Available accounts indicate he did not arrive in Washington, D.C., until Sunday, September 15. He notified his sisters of his safe arrival there in a letter dated September 17. This circumstance also reveals a window of opportunity, between September 8 and 15, during which John may have visited Kate Hewitt. In a letter to his sisters Reynolds stated, "by Saturday's mail I rec'd orders to join the Army of the Potomac, and left that afternoon reaching here on Sunday (by way of Baltimore)." One is left to wonder where Reynolds was on Saturday, September 14, when he received these orders. Apparently, he was either in Philadelphia visiting his sister Kate or in Baltimore staying with his sister Jennie. Either way, these orders called for him to "repair to Washington, via Baltimore, by Steamer 'S.R. Spaulding.'" Thus, it seems Reynolds may have been in Philadelphia on September 14, traveled by train to Baltimore and then went on to Washington via steamer. Regardless, there was certainly time for him to visit Kate between the time he departed Fort Trumbull and the time he boarded the SS *Spaulding*.[131]

In any event, native Pennsylvanian Brigadier General John Reynolds's assignment with the Army of the Potomac seemed perfectly apropos as he assumed command of the First Brigade of the Pennsylvania Reserve Division. (The division comprised three brigades.) Between September 1861 and the spring of 1862, Reynolds found himself involved in a number of actions and spent time as the military commander of Fredericksburg, Virginia.

Reynolds did have at least one respite; it came during January 1862. Able to travel freely to Washington, he rode into town to visit his brother William and his wife, Rebecca, who were temporarily visiting the nation's capital. Edward Nichols, in *Toward Gettysburg*, indicates the first in what became a series of visits with his older brother and his wife took place on January 11. Two of John's sisters, Ellie and Kate, also expressed an interest in traveling to D.C. in order to partake in the family camaraderie, but Reynolds warned them of an outbreak of smallpox and typhoid fever in the area and was concerned, especially for his sister Kate, who had planned to bring her children. Be that as it may, it appears that Ellie and John's sister Hal did come. The length of time within which these series of family visits took place is not certain. But with Reynolds stationed within riding distance, he apparently made a number of trips into town to see his family. In one note, Reynolds indicated that he planned to visit with his family again in Washington on January 18, so it appears the time frame of the visits extended at least from January 11 to 18. Certainly, Kate Hewitt must have been on Reynolds's mind too. Perhaps he took similar advantage of his proximity to Washington, D.C., during this period of

Right: John Reynolds as a brigadier general of volunteers. *Library of Congress.*

Below: One of the regiments originally attached to the First Brigade of the Pennsylvania Reserves Division, the Thirtieth Pennsylvania Volunteer Infantry (previously the First Pennsylvania Reserve Regiment). *Library of Congress.*

time to rendezvous with Kate Hewitt. If so, there is no available evidence to point to such a visit.[132]

It was not until June 1862 that John Reynolds saw what was at the time, his most formidable action of the war. This was during the Union army's Peninsula Campaign under General George McClellan, the so-called Young Napoleon. Beginning in March 1862, McClellan moved most of the Army of the Potomac from northern Virginia, via the Potomac River and Chesapeake Bay, to Fort Monroe in Hampton, Virginia (at the confluence of the James and York Rivers, adjacent to the mouth of the Chesapeake Bay and the Atlantic Ocean). McClellan planned to threaten Richmond, the capital of the Confederacy, and the Confederate army protecting it, by moving up the peninsula separating the York and James Rivers. The general's habitual overestimation of opposing forces, which was largely based on faulty intelligence reports, slowed his willingness to confront the enemy. Finally in late May, McClellan attacked the Confederates in a battle that came to be known as the Battle of Seven Pines. An inconsequential affair, strategically, the battle could not have been of greater consequence, as the Confederate army commander Joseph E. Johnston was wounded and his place was taken by the indomitable Robert E. Lee. Within a month, Lee's forces clashed with McClellan's army in a series of battles later known as the Seven Days' Battles. The Pennsylvania Reserves joined McClellan's forces in early June, just in time for these battles. Arriving in theater by June 11, Reynolds and the men of the Pennsylvania Reserves were finally in position to make their mark.[133]

In this, their first major action of the U.S. Civil War, the Pennsylvanians did well, and John Reynolds's star shone brightly. In fact, during the Battle of Mechanicsville, it seemed as if all of the lessons Reynolds had learned at West Point, during the Mexican War and throughout his twenty years of military experience had combined to ensure his success. The Pennsylvania Reserves Division, operating under General George A. McCall (recall Reynolds commanded one of three brigades in this division), were part of Fitz John Porter's newly created Fifth Corps. Porter's corps held the right flank of the Union line, and McCall's division of Pennsylvanians manned the extreme right of the corps' line along the banks of Beaver Dam Creek. In anticipation of battle, Reynolds prepared his line of defense and deployed his troops and associated artillery in optimal positions. General Porter, in reflecting on his inspection of Reynolds's line, indicated he had "the best reasons not only to be contented, but thoroughly gratified with the admirable arrangements of this accomplished officer." The position was a strong one with cleared fields of fire to the front, abatis (felled timber with sharpened edges) protecting the troops, plenty of supporting artillery and reserve forces nearby. Famed Confederate artillerist and engineer Edward Porter Alexander later called the position "absolutely impregnable to a front attack." It's a good thing that it was, as protecting the army's flank was of vital importance. Put simply, if Reynolds's men failed, the Union army would be in serious trouble.[134]

The Confederates attacked late on the afternoon of June 26. During the battle, Reynolds's and Seymour's brigades of Pennsylvania Reserves were hit by forces led by Generals A.P. Hill, D.H. Hill and James Longstreet. The fighting was fierce, but Reynolds's leadership combined with the excellent defensive position occupied by his men proved to be the difference makers. By the end of the day, the reserves, aided handsomely by three batteries of artillery (eighteen cannons), had held off elements of two Confederate divisions and doled out an estimated three to four times the amount of casualties they had suffered. Throughout it all, Reynolds seemed fearless, frequently placing himself in harm's way. Yet somehow he avoided enemy bullets. It seemed as though John Reynolds was invincible.[135]

But as "a bright and clear day" with "light breezes" dawned on June 27, the Union army fell back into a new defensive position in an area known as Gaines' Mill. Reynolds's men and the rest of the division were to be held in reserve this day. But it was not to be. The ferocious fighting that day soon necessitated a call for all hands, and as a result Reynolds led his men into the fray. Time and again he could be seen at the front, deploying and redeploying his men as dictated by the ebb and flow of battle. Once again, Reynolds and his men fought valiantly, but this time they suffered significant casualties. Despite their stalwart efforts and those of their brothers in arms, the Union army was forced to retreat. In the aftermath of

Alfred Waud's drawing captures the action in the vicinity of Reynolds's front during the Battle of Mechanicsville (also known as the Battle of Beaver Dam Creek). *Library of Congress.*

the day's fighting, there was much confusion. Late that evening, in seeking to select the best ground to redeploy artillery, Reynolds found himself not only isolated from the main line with a wounded horse but also stuck in the midst of a swamp. Stranded there overnight, he quickly sought refuge the following morning. But by then, the enemy had gotten behind the former Union line, and with this, Reynolds could not avoid capture. As localized thunderstorms raged that evening, they amplified John's dour mood at having become a prisoner of war.[136]

John Reynolds's time as a guest of the Confederacy proved relatively short, as he was exchanged for a Confederate officer six weeks later. Though Reynolds was initially placed in the comfortable confines of Richmond's Spotswood Hotel, he spent the latter part of his captivity at Libby Prison in Richmond, Virginia. While at Libby, he suffered some degree of hardship. However, his experience as a captured Union officer paled in comparison to the conditions experienced by other Union soldiers captured later in the war, especially those sent to Libby.[137]

Soon after his return to the Army of the Potomac, Reynolds received command of the entire Pennsylvania Reserve Division, at the time roughly seven thousand men. By then it was August 1862. Before long, Reynolds's skills as a division commander would be tested in the Battle of Second Bull Run (Second Manassas). Once again, Reynolds proved more than ready for the test.[138]

John Reynolds's actions at Second Bull Run represent some of his finest as a soldier and leader. On the heels of his success outside of Richmond, Robert E. Lee moved his Army of Northern Virginia north to intercept another Union force. This was the newly constituted Union Army of Virginia, under General John Pope. General McClellan was supposed to relocate his army as quickly as possible to assist Pope, but he dragged his feet. Reynolds and the Pennsylvania Reserves, after a march of nearly thirty miles, were attached to Pope's army. Despite John's earnest efforts, his troops did not see heavy fighting until the last day of the three-day battle. By then, Pope had failed miserably as a field commander, and as a result his army was retreating. It is not too much to say that Pope's army's survival depended on the troops covering their retreat. Fortunately for Pope and his army, this unenviable task fell to Reynolds's division and a few other hard-fighting groups of Union soldiers.[139]

Certainly, other Union troops fought as well as the Pennsylvanians that day; some may even have fought better. But the actions of the Pennsylvania Reserves on Henry House Hill deserve notice, as they contributed significantly

Edwin Forbes sketch portraying the moment when two brigades of Reynolds's Pennsylvania Reserves (Meade and Seymour) marched to support Pope's left flank on Henry House Hill. *Library of Congress.*

to covering Pope's army in its retreat. And some accounts credit their success, at least in part, to Reynolds's leadership. His troops were positioned on Henry House Hill, not far from the spot that the legendary Confederate "Stonewall Jackson" had earned his sobriquet during the First Battle of Bull Run just over a year prior. Once again, during the late afternoon of August 30, 1862, important actions between Union and Confederate forces played out on this storied piece of real estate. But this time, it was the Union troops that would be remembered for their stalwart stand and their heroism. And a number of accounts place Reynolds in the midst of the mêlée.[140]

As events unfolded late in the afternoon of what had been a sultry summer day, Reynolds received an urgent call to position two brigades from his division on the hill. His men were not alone in this effort, as a brigade of U.S. regulars from General George W. Sykes's Fifth Corps were sent to assist Reynolds in securing the hill along with Milroy's independent brigade. At least three batteries of artillery supported these troops, and additional troops would be summoned to assist before the fighting ended. Though the hill and the partially sunken Manassas-Sudley Road offered Reynolds's men a degree of protection, the position was precarious. The Union troops were placed on Henry House Hill in a critical effort to protect the Union army's avenue of retreat over the destined-to-be-infamous Stone Bridge that spanned Bull

Run (creek). This bridge was the army's primary escape route. Were it to be lost, the army might be destroyed. The task of protecting the bridge was made more than difficult as the opposing troops under Confederate general James Longstreet could taste not only victory but the annihilation of the Union army as well. Indeed, his men sought to capitalize on their already successful efforts that day by gaining control of the Stone Bridge and nearby river fords in order to sever Pope's line of retreat. But Reynolds's men and troops from George Sykes's brigades refused to let that happen.[141]

When Longstreet's men hit, they struck in an orderly yet intense manner. The fight for the hill started at Reynolds's end of the Union line. Here, the Pennsylvania Reserves had the responsibility of holding down the right flank of the line. The initial action pitted Reynolds and his men against Colonel Henry "Rock" Benning's brigade of General D.R. Jones's division, Longstreet's Corps. The boys in blue not only held steady but also soon exploited an unfolding opportunity as Benning and his men inadvertently exposed their flank to the reserves. Only three hundred yards separated the opposing forces, and in a flash Reynolds seized the moment. Spurring his horse to the front of Meade's brigade (one of the two brigades of his division in position on the hill), Reynolds grabbed the flag of the Second Pennsylvania Reserves in an impetuous effort to inspire his men. Waving the staff furiously, he yelled to his troops, "Now boys, give them the steel, charge bayonets, double quick!" Perhaps it was foolhardy, certainly it was risky, but John Reynolds was not about to see his troops miss the opportunity to stop the enemy forces. One eyewitness account captured the moment: "Reynolds, ever alert, driving his spurs into his horse's side, shouted his order: 'Forward Reserves!' In a moment his troops, inoculated with his enthusiasm, swept forward and downward." As his men approached the Georgians' flank, Reynolds was an easy mark for Rebel marksmen, but as the eyewitness observed, "he seemed to bear a charmed life." But the question begged, how long could Reynolds defy the odds?[142]

The Georgians bravely turned to face Reynolds and the reserves. Soon they were joined by other forces in the attack on the Union line. As fighting erupted all along the line, the situation became desperate for the Yankees. Both sides sought and received reinforcements. During one critical moment, another brigade, Robert C. Buchanan's U.S. regulars, arrived to buttress the Union line. Though the Confederates worked around the left flank of the Union line, the boys in blue hung on against seemingly overwhelming numbers. In the midst of the tumultuous situation, Reynolds, once again, threw caution to the wind. This time grabbing the flagstaff of the Sixth

Pennsylvania Reserves, Reynolds spurred his charger all along his line, earnestly urging his men to hold their position. Before the fighting ended, the Confederates had missed a golden opportunity to make the most of their flanking movement against the left end of the Union line. But the fighting had been fierce, and the onset of darkness helped foster an end to the battle for Henry House Hill. Fortunately (for the Union army), Reynolds's Pennsylvania Reserves, Sykes's men, their supporting artillery and some additional reinforcements succeeded in holding off the men in butternut and gray. Pope's line of retreat was secured and his army saved. Later, the official records made clear where the credit was due: "Sykes with his disciplined brigades and Reynolds, with his gallant Pennsylvania Reserves, seized the commanding ground in rear, and like a rock, withstood the advance of the victorious army and saved the union from rout." One wonders if the "like a rock" comment was a touché reference to the hill's previous connection to Stonewall Jackson. Regardless, Reynolds and his men certainly proved their mettle on Henry House Hill.[143]

14

JOHN

CIVIL WAR—CORPS COMMAND

His head thrown back…his great black eyes flashing fire,
he was everywhere upon the field.

D uring the U.S. Civil War, there was no rest for the weary. Not long
after Second Bull Run, John Reynolds was detached from the
Army of the Potomac (against his wishes) and sent to Harrisburg,
Pennsylvania, as requested by Governor Curtain, to command state militia.
This was in response to the Confederate "invasion" that came to be known
as the Antietam Campaign. Aside from duty concerns, this assignment did
have one advantage, as it might have afforded Reynolds an opportunity to
visit Kate Hewitt. However, no documentation exists to indicate he did so.
In fact, Kate's whereabouts at the time remain uncertain.

Shortly after the Battle of Antietam, Reynolds returned to the Army
of the Potomac (now roughly 120,000 men) and was placed in temporary
command of the First Army Corps due to Major General Joseph Hooker's
wounding at Antietam. Reynolds received a promotion to major general on
November 29, 1862, and just two weeks later led his corps during the Battle
of Fredericksburg in December 1862.[144]

Fredericksburg marked Major General John Reynolds's first battle
in command of a corps (about 18,500 men at the time of the battle).
Once again, the Army of the Potomac found itself under a new overall
commander; this time it was Ambrose Burnside. Reynolds experienced
a lot of frustration at Fredericksburg, much of it due to the cumbersome
command structure then in place and some of it from within his own corps.

Army of the Potomac commanding officer Major General Ambrose Burnside (*seated, center of image*) and various officers, including Brigadier General John Reynolds (*standing over Burnside's left shoulder*). In a late November 1862 letter he wrote soon after the photo was taken (just prior to his promotion), Reynolds informed his sisters that the photo was "very good," telling them "if you can ever get a copy of it, do so." *Courtesy of Archives and Special Collections, Franklin and Marshall College, Lancaster, Pennsylvania.*

The battle opened on December 13, a warmer day than one might expect for that time of year—temperatures approached the mid-fifties. Reynolds's men were positioned on the army's left flank. Their job was to cross the Rappahannock River in order to threaten the Confederate army's right flank. That meant butting heads with Stonewall Jackson's corps. This was no easy task. Reynolds's chances for success were foiled from the beginning by his superiors' unwillingness to strike with overwhelming force despite earlier indications that they would do just that. Also complicating things was the fact that any opportunity for surprise was lost due to the late arrival of pontoons to facilitate a timely river crossing. Finally, the Confederate forces at that end of the line enjoyed the advantage of a panoramic view of the battlefield from Prospect Hill. Unfortunately for Reynolds's men, Jackson's forces could see what was coming.[145]

However, despite the Confederates' advantages, the initial results were somewhat surprising. Reynolds's forces, notably Meade's Division of the

Alfred Waud's sketch of the pontoon bridges erected for Reynolds's Corps. Unfortunately for the Union forces, the late arrival of the bridge-building supplies foreshadowed Reynolds's forthcoming attack. *Library of Congress.*

Pennsylvania Reserves as well as others, penetrated Jackson's line. But after this initial progress, Jackson's men rallied as the First Corps units could not maintain the ground they had gained. Aside from having an advantage in numbers, Jackson's forces had the advantage of a strong defensive position. By the time Reynolds sent reinforcements from his own corps to support the reserves, it was too late. Support sent from other corps arrived too late as well. Casualties were heavy on Reynolds's front, and worse yet, it all proved for naught. In reflecting on the battle, Reynolds expressed a degree of disappointment in his corps during the engagement, "My Corps, or two Divisions of it, made the attack on the left, and after almost gaining the object let it slip, they did not do as well as I expected." In fairness, the effectiveness of Reynolds's own performance in his first battle as corps commander has drawn some debate. Be that as it may, at least one eyewitness indicated Reynolds had not only looked the part of a successful corps commander but acted the part as well: "Mounted upon a superb black horse, with his head thrown back and his great black eyes flashing fire, he was every where [*sic*] upon the field, seeing all things and giving commands in person." Certainly, commanding an army corps was altogether different from commanding a division. Regardless, Reynolds gained invaluable experience. Moreover, he saw clear evidence that the timeless adage "He who hesitates is lost" held true as much, if not more, in warfare as it did in life. And he also learned that there was no substitute for entering into a battle with overwhelming force. Perhaps all of this set the stage for his actions in the next battle in which his men would have an opportunity to lead the way. Thus, it seems the Battle of Fredericksburg had offered many lessons to John Reynolds.[146]

On the heels of Fredericksburg, during late December 1862 (a day or so after Christmas), Reynolds traveled to Philadelphia on leave. While there, he visited his family and also took time to call on Margaretta Meade, wife of General Meade, and her family. Apparently, Reynolds was back in camp by January 3, 1863, so this was a quick trip. Be that as it may, if he had time to see his family and Mrs. Meade and her family, he likely had time to visit Kate Hewitt, if she had remained in the vicinity. There is some evidence, albeit circumstantial, to indicate she did so, but unfortunately no records can be found to shed light on any such visit.[147]

Before the spring campaign season, Reynolds found one more opportunity to visit Philadelphia. On February 24, John wrote to his sister Ellie, "I hope to be able to run on to Phila next week but am not certain when." Per John, he was awaiting Meade's return from Philadelphia before he could leave. Fortunately for Reynolds, Meade returned in time for him to begin a ten-day furlough on February 27, 1863. Interestingly, this was on the heels of Valentine's Day. With this, it certainly represented a good opportunity for Reynolds to visit not only family but Kate as well.[148]

Meanwhile, the Union army's defeat at Fredericksburg represented another disappointment to the Lincoln administration. And this pointed to a possible change in command for the hapless Army of the Potomac. In this case, the change came a month later, after Burnside's failed offensive known to history as the bloodless yet calamitous "Mud March." Soon after this debacle, army commander General Ambrose Burnside was relieved of duty as commanding officer of the struggling Army of the Potomac. Next man "up to bat" in the Union army's failed command "hit parade" was Major General Hooker.

During early May 1863, General Hooker led the Army of the Potomac into its first battle under his command. Reynolds experienced much exasperation during this battle, as the First Corps was more or less held in reserve during the Army of the Potomac's first large battle of the campaign season, the Battle of Chancellorsville. The circumstances surrounding his corps' inaction frustrated Reynolds to no end and may very well have influenced his inclination to make certain his troops never again missed their opportunity for battle, though this is only speculation. In the end, Chancellorsville proved yet another ignominious defeat for the Army of the Potomac. Conversely, it was perhaps Lee's greatest victory. As a result, it was General Hooker's turn to meet with disgrace. Though Hooker's strategic and organizational skills proved sound, his abilities to command in the heat of battle fell short. Worst of all, at a critical moment during the battle he apparently lost his nerve. With his army's defeat, the nation's commander in chief, President Lincoln, lost faith in Hooker. Soon after, the president set his mind to finding an able replacement.[149]

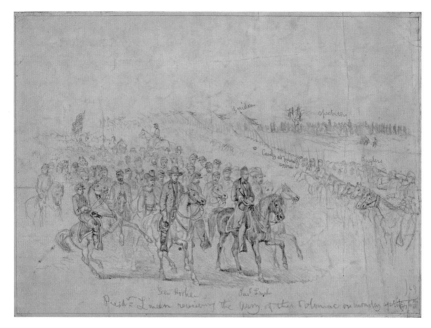

This drawing by Edwin Forbes provides a rendition of President Lincoln reviewing the Army of the Potomac Cavalry Corps on Monday, April 6, 1863. In a letter to his sister written just a few days afterward, General Reynolds indicated that he was among the group that dined with President Lincoln that evening and that Lincoln reviewed his corps separately (some corps were reviewed together) on April 9. Reynolds also remarked, "If the Troops only fight as well as they looked, no expectation however great, need be disappointed." *Library of Congress.*

In the meantime, John Reynolds's ascendancy through command had drawn the attention of Lincoln. As a result, on the cusp of the commencement of the Gettysburg Campaign, President Abraham Lincoln offered John Reynolds overall command of the Army of the Potomac. This offer came during Reynolds's visit with Lincoln on June 2, 1863. The offer was quite an honor, but unless he was given free rein as the army commander, unbridled from armchair commanders in Washington, D.C., including the president, Reynolds preferred to remain in a subordinate role. Reynolds had seen the pitfalls of armies held under the thumb of politicians, dating back to the Mexican War and throughout the Civil War, and he wanted no part of it. But Lincoln could not guarantee him the free hand he sought. With this, Reynolds demurred. For the time being, Hooker maintained command of the Army of the Potomac.[150]

Reynolds's fateful meeting with President Lincoln took place less than thirty days before his date with destiny at Gettysburg. As is normally the case, it can be a blessing for one not to know the future. Unaware of what fate held for him, Reynolds took full advantage of his proximity to family after his meeting with the president. Traveling directly to Baltimore, he visited his sisters Ellie and Jennie that evening. (Ellie was visiting Jennie, who lived in Baltimore with her husband.) He departed the next day to rejoin the army. In considering all of this, he may have also had time to meet with Kate during this period. But here again, no documentation exists to indicate whether or not he did so.

This 1863 drawing of President Abraham Lincoln portrays the president as he would likely have appeared when he met with General Reynolds on June 2, 1863. *Library of Congress.*

On June 12, as the Confederate army moved northward from Virginia toward Maryland and Pennsylvania, Hooker placed Reynolds in command of the "right wing" of the Army of the Potomac. This action put Reynolds in overall command of four army corps to include the First Corps (his corps), Third (Sickles), Fifth (Meade's) Corps, Eleventh (Howard's) Corps and the cavalry (Pleasonton). But by June 25, with Union forces well into Maryland (and Confederates in Pennsylvania), Reynolds had received a new assignment, command of the "left wing" of the Army of the Potomac to include three corps of infantry, the First, Third, Eleventh and a brigade of cavalry. With this, Reynolds commanded some thirty thousand men.[151]

Interestingly, Reynolds found time a few days later, while in Frederick, Maryland, to visit a cousin who lived in Frederick. As with all the other windows of opportunity in which Reynolds might have stolen a few

Max Rosenthal's portrait of General Reynolds shows him as a major general with two stars on each shoulder board and the requisite number of buttons worn by an officer of this rank (sixteen). *Library of Congress.*

This exceptionally rare image, taken by CJ Tyson, circa 1867–68, clearly shows a tree carved with the initial *R* (for Reynolds) to indicate the area where General Reynolds was killed. *Boardman Collection.*

moments with Kate Hewitt, one is left to wonder if he did so at this time. Either way, almost certainly this was his last opportunity to do so. With this, the die was cast for the tragedy that was about to befall the secret engagement of Kate Hewitt and John Reynolds.[152]

On June 28, 1863, President Lincoln finally relieved Hooker of command and ordered General Meade to assume command of the Army of the Potomac. And as the Union army gradually approached the crossroads town of Gettysburg from the south, the troops also provided a screen between the Confederate forces and the nation's capital and other major Northern cities of consequence (particularly Baltimore and Philadelphia). As fate would have it, Reynolds's left wing was located closest to Gettysburg and, in turn,

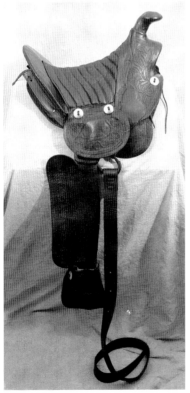

Above: This kepi (cap) was worn by Major General John Fulton Reynolds, USA, when he was killed at the Battle of Gettysburg on July 1, 1863 (note: The buttons and chinstrap are not original to the kepi). *Courtesy of the National Park Service, Gettysburg National Military Park, GETT 44742.*

Left: This is the saddle on which Major General John Fulton Reynolds was killed at the Battle of Gettysburg, July 1, 1863. Reynolds likely acquired this nineteenth-century Mexican-style riding saddle during his pre–Civil War military career, which included service in the Mexican-American War of 1846–47. *Courtesy of the National Park Service, Gettysburg National Military Park, GETT 45397.*

the Confederate army. And as we have seen, John Reynolds's destiny soon placed him squarely in the bull's eye of a Confederate bullet at Gettysburg.[153]

Sadly, this brave leader with a penchant for placing himself in perilous positions during the heat of battle met his demise at Gettysburg. With Reynolds's untimely death, his legacy was sealed. A bona-fide war hero, fearless leader and stalwart defender of the nation to which he swore an oath, Major General John Fulton Reynolds made the ultimate sacrifice at Gettysburg. He, along with General Buford, had chosen to make a stand west of the town. And though the Union army suffered a tactical defeat by the end of the first day's fighting, they won a strategic victory. The high ground Buford and Reynolds protected, south and east of town, by choosing to defend the ground west and north of town on July 1, positioned General Meade well for the victory he secured over the next two days of fighting.[154]

But victories can be costly, and Gettysburg was no exception. In actuality, it proved to be the rule. John Reynolds's death serves as a clear example of the tragedy and sacrifice of the battle. His loss proved almost unbearable to his brothers in arms, friends and family. But above all, the news of his death devastated the love of his life, Kate Hewitt. As with anyone who has lost their true love, her grief was beyond words. What would she do now? She had lost the man she loved and planned to marry. Yet she had never even met his family because her engagement to him had been a secret. Sadly, they had planned to announce their engagement to his family in Philadelphia on July 8, 1863. And there was one more thing. Kate had made a certain promise to John, but the question was, would she keep it?

15

KATE

FAREWELL JOHN

We feel so for her, tis like crushing the life out of her.

Ellie Reynolds wrote to her brother, naval officer William Reynolds, on Sunday, July 5, 1863, "Yesterday, the anniversary of our country's birth, we consigned to the grave the body of our dear one who has given up his life for his & our country. This will not be the first announcement to you of John's fate; you will have seen it, as we did, in the paper." The news of John Reynolds's death reached Philadelphia quickly. The local papers conveyed the news surrounding the death of Pennsylvania's native son as early as the 5:00 a.m. edition of the *Philadelphia Inquirer* of July 2. In a short article detailing the commencement of fighting at Gettysburg on July 1, under the headline, "First Battles in Pennsylvania," the *Inquirer* dutifully announced, in equally bold letters, "Maj-Gen. Reynolds Killed." And apparently that announcement, or one like it, reached not only John's family and all the concerned citizens of Philadelphia but also the beautiful twenty-seven-year-old woman who had professed her love and undying commitment to John Reynolds: Kate Hewitt. Thus Kate learned that the man to whom she was engaged to be married had been struck down by a Confederate bullet at Gettysburg.[155]

It has often been said that fate is a cruel hunter. Sadly, for Kate Hewitt and John Reynolds, fate came hunting for John on the first day of a battle that would ultimately take thousands of lives. Be that as it may, there was only one death at Gettysburg that mattered to Kate Hewitt. And that was the

SECOND EDITION.

FIVE O'CLOCK A. M.

THE INVASION.

THE FIRST BATTLE ON PENNSYL- VANIA SOIL.

Gens. Longstreet, Hill, Reynolds, and Meade, Engaged near Gettysburg.

THE FIGHT VERY SEVERE.

HEAVY LOSS.

GENERAL REYNOLDS KILLED.

IMPORTANT FROM HARRISBURG.

STRENGTH OF THE REBEL ARMY.

Lee has over 98,000 Men and 210 Pieces of Artillery.

Stuart's Cavalry not Included.

Movements of the Rebel Generals.

Heavy Firing in the Direction of Dillsburg.

A Fierce Engagement at Hanover.

1,800 CONTEND WITH 6,000.

CAPTURE OF A SOUTH CAROLINA RE-GIMENT AND THREE GUNS.

NEW YORK, July 2—4 o'clock A. M.—The New York *Times* has just received the following important despatch, dated near GETTYSBURG, Pa., July 1.—The first heavy engagement on Pennsylvania soil was commenced at 9 o'clock this morning, between the rebels under Generals Long-street and Hill, and the First and Eleventh Corps under Generals Meade and Reynolds. The locality of the battle is beyond Get-tysburg, on the Chambersburg pike.

Portions of the fight have been very se-vere and attended with heavy loss. Thus far, the onset of the enemy has been suc-cessfully resisted by the two corps men-tioned.

The Third and Twelfth Corps are coming up.

I regret to say that Major General Rey-nolds was mortally wounded, and has since died.

death of the man she had met at the very moment she set out to turn her life around. As mentioned previously, after leaving a checkered past behind in California, Kate's successful conversion to Catholicism impressed Eden Hall administrators so much that it was lauded as "remarkable." Seldom if ever were individual students mentioned in such a light. But Kate stirred something in the souls of those in charge at Eden Hall. In the same way, she stirred something in John's heart when they met aboard the SS *Golden Age* during the summer of 1860. To be sure, Kate's commitment to both John and her faith reached their zenith when she promised him, likely on the occasion of their betrothal, that she would enter a religious life should he be killed during the war.[156]

On July 3, 1863, at "nearly 2:00 a.m.," John Reynolds's remains arrived at the home of his sister Kate and her husband, Henry "Harry" Landis, in Philadelphia. The casket was "metal painted to look like rosewood," and it was set upon the family's breakfast table, which in turn was placed in "the parlor in front of the mantel." A clear glass plate on the casket allowed the family a limited glimpse at their fallen loved one.[157]

As the family grieved and received flowers and sentiments from numerous mourners, Kate Hewitt surely wrestled with her emotions. Every bone in her body must have

This Philadelphia newspaper account of the fighting at Gettysburg announced the fall of General Reynolds at Gettysburg. This article, or one like it, likely served as Kate Hewitt's first notice that her beloved fiancé had been killed. *From the* Philadelphia Press, *Second Edition, July 2, 1863 (GenealogyBank.com).*

John Reynolds's remains arrived at the home of his sister, Catharine Reynolds Landis, at approximately 2:00 a.m. on July 2, 1863. This modern-day view of the steps to her home, located at 1829 Spruce Street (adjacent to Philadelphia's famed Rittenhouse Square), shows the entryway much as it would have appeared at the time. *Courtesy of Kim Chantry.*

yearned to see the earthly remains of the love of her life one last time. Quite simply, Kate needed closure. Yet knowing the family had been totally unaware of her engagement to John, she hesitated. According to Jennie, in a letter written to her brother William, who was unable to attend John's funeral as a result of his duties with the navy, "as she knew no one of the family she thought she ought not to come, but felt she could not resist the wish to see him again."[158]

Sadly, per Ellie, "She had been expecting John to meet her in Phila. On the 8 of July & she said there he was to bring her to us." This meeting was assuredly to announce their engagement. But fate dictated otherwise. Now she would finally meet the family, but not in the way she had envisioned. The dream of meeting John and announcing their engagement had turned into a nightmare.[159]

While Kate tried to come to grips with the devastating news of John's death and her angst over what to do about seeing his remains, John's family suffered with their grief as well. The family was also curious and somewhat intrigued regarding some of John's personal effects, especially a few mysterious letters, a small ring and two Catholic treasures on a silken cord. As Jennie indicated, "Around his neck was a little heart and medal. We all thought a lady was the donor and must be prized and wished we could only know who & where she was." But there was more. "In the valise were two letters from Eden Hall (Torrisdale?) [sic] signed Kate." Jennie continued, "Several of her pictures were in the valise. Her letters were sealed with his class ring, and on his finger was one with 'dear Kate' inside." Equally as perplexing, John's West Point class ring was missing. Had Reynolds lost it? Did it fall off his finger when his aides hastily removed him from the battlefield? Had it been left behind when his body was embalmed in Baltimore? Perhaps it was lost when his body was encased in ice, in Union Bridge, Maryland. Or maybe it went missing when his body had been placed in a crude, undersized box in Gettysburg.[160]

So while Kate battled with her grief and indecision about visiting John's family, John's sisters struggled similarly with their grief and the uncertainty surrounding John's belongings. Ironically, the answers to these questions were, both literally and figuratively, right around the corner. Jennie conveyed the moment of Kate's arrival, "Friday morning a note came up stairs saying Mr. Ewing & Miss Hewitt wished to see the remains if agreeable. Ellie asked 'is she Kate.' [sic] 'Yes.' So she & Hal went to receive her." As Jennie's description of Kate's arrival at the family home continued, she conveyed to her brother William a succinct but extremely descriptive image of the family's emotional state on learning about Kate: "I need not tell you what a thunder clap it was to us all."[161]

This image shows Kate Hewitt as she likely appeared in the early 1860s. A period ink inscription on the back of the image that appears to be in the hand of Rebecca Reynolds (William Reynolds's wife) identifies Kate and is dated December 19, 1863. The significance of this date is unclear. It seems unlikely Kate posed on this date, as, only six months after John's death, she would probably be dressed in mourning. This opens up the possibility that she sat for this portrait at an earlier time and a copy was given to Rebecca, or that it was another copy print, much like the portrait of young Kate. It can fairly be stated that the likeness dates between the fall of 1860 and December 1863. *Courtesy of Archives and Special Collections, Franklin and Marshall College, Lancaster, Pennsylvania, caption developed in conjunction with R. Coddington and E. Topping of* Military Images *magazine.*

To their credit, John Reynolds's sisters welcomed Kate Hewitt with open arms. Their descriptions of Kate are warm, poignant, heartfelt, sympathetic and quite informative. In turn, if not for Ellie's and Jennie's letters to their brother William, far less would be known of John's and Kate's relationship and of Kate herself. Ellie wrote of Kate's emotions: "She had not shed a tear till she entered the parlor and then she wept copiously on her knees beside him." Ellie continued, "At night she was very calm & so we sat beside him. She would say in the sweetest, saddest voice, 'Dearest.' & once or twice, 'Dearest, how can I give you up.' 'Dearest, it is very hard to give you up.'" Ellie also quoted Kate's account of what had happened to John's West Point class ring: "I promised when he put this ring on my finger, I would <u>never</u> take it off till <u>he</u> did it & now I will give him up to his God & take it off." Ellie then informed William, "She kissed it & put it on the glass plate. It was a great struggle. She said she could not keep it as a Sister of Charity & she must give it all up now." And there was more: "As she laid the ring down she said, 'Never let it be tainted by a disloyal hand. He was too true for that.'" Ellie then detailed how Kate "asked for the little relic & said that she could keep [it]." Presumably this "relic" was the cross and heart that Jennie had indicated Reynolds had worn around his neck.[162]

Meanwhile, Jennie informed William how John and Kate met: "Four years ago they met coming from California (I think in 1860)." She described Kate this way, "You would be pleased with her letters. They show such a delicate, refined mind so far above ordinary love epistles…" and "She is a lady of means." And though her Victorian morals tugged at her conscience,

This etching depicts members of the Reynolds family and Kate Hewitt visiting the battlefield in Gettysburg during November 1863. This remarkable work was created by the late Anne Hoffman Cleaver, great-granddaughter of John Reynolds's sister Lydia Moore (Reynolds) Evans. Cleaver based the etching on a rare photograph owned by the family that shows members of the family with Kate near the foot of Little Round Top (in an area dubbed the "Slaughter Pen"). Research and analysis of the photo on which the etching was based and an extant photograph of Kate Hewitt indicates she is likely the woman in the middle of the group. *Courtesy of Katie Cleaver.*

Jennie could not resist a comment regarding Kate's beauty: "I won't send a personal description. You would not be disappointed if you saw her, but we ought not to judge of looks under such circumstances."[163]

Ultimately, Ellie's and Jennie's letters served to touch the heart. Their collective outpouring of love for their brother still resonates through their letters 159 years later. It is obvious in reading these letters that John Reynolds

This image, per information gleaned from a Reynolds family descendant photo album, corresponding research and photo analysis, shows Kate Hewitt along with Reynolds family members on the battlefield near the "Devils Den" during November 1863. Kate Hewitt is believed to be the second woman from the left. Reynolds family members also present in the image include John Reynolds's sister Kate and her husband, Harry Landis, as well as Reynolds's sisters Ellie, Jennie and Hal. *Courtesy of Katie Cleaver.*

meant the world to his family but perhaps most especially to Ellie and Jennie. Beyond this, as mentioned previously, Ellie's and Jennie's letters to William clearly demonstrate their sincere sympathies for Kate. Moreover, it seems as though they opened their hearts to her without hesitation and they did so in the most earnest and endearing way possible. Meanwhile, Jennie's short yet poignant line of prose speaks volumes with regard to her and Ellie's sympathies for Kate, while at the same time describing what a devastating and crippling loss John's death was for Kate: "We feel so for her, 'tis like crushing the life out of her."[164]

Finally, one more crucial piece of information emerges from Jennie's letter to William: "She had his consent to enter a religious life should she lose him and now she intends to do it, as the world has no interest for her now." There it was, the last promise Kate had made to John, a promise she would earnestly try to keep. Be that as it may, fate, once again, had plans for Kate Hewitt that she likely never expected.[165]

16

KATE

THE DAUGHTERS OF CHARITY—EMMITSBURG

Her position is a settled one & she feels at home in her duties.

The Daughters of Charity community finds its roots in Paris, France, in 1633. Founded by Saint Vincent de Paul and Saint Louise de Marillac, the Daughters of Charity mission centered on a group of young women dedicated to the care of the sick and the poor. Unlike similar groups of the time that normally led cloistered lives and seldom interacted with the less fortunate of the French populace, the Daughters of Charity sisters often lived and worked among those they served. In point of fact, these sisters' hallmark came in the form of soup kitchens for the destitute, schools for orphans (with a focus on teaching the young to read and write), hospitals for the ill and infirm and prison reform for inmates.[166]

Over two hundred years later, the Daughters of Charity community inspired America's own Elizabeth Ann Seton. Born into a prominent New York Episcopal family, Seton married by age nineteen but lost her husband to tuberculosis after only nine years of marriage. A widow with five children, she converted to Catholicism not long after her husband's death.[167]

Sharing the same concerns for the less fortunate as the Daughters of Charity, Elizabeth Seton's passion for Catholicism led her to establish the first such community for religious women in the United States, in Emmitsburg, Maryland, in 1809. The community came to be known as the Sisters of Charity of St. Joseph's. Within a year, the community also established Saint Joseph's Academy and Free School for Catholic girls, the country's first free Catholic school. Just over a century and a half later, Elizabeth Ann Seton would become known to the world as the first person born in what would become the United States to be canonized by the Catholic Church as Saint Elizabeth Ann Seton. Meanwhile, the community she founded in Emmitsburg was merged with the French Daughters of Charity in 1850 and has been known by that name ever since.[168]

Emmitsburg itself proved an ideal setting for Elizabeth Seton's school and religious community. Founded in 1785 and incorporated in 1825, the town remained a sleepy little farm community throughout the nineteenth century. Located on the Maryland and Pennsylvania border, the town is nestled on the edge of the South Mountain foothills. The bucolic setting surrounding the town offered residents and visitors alike a peaceful and enjoyable environment in which to raise a family. This ideal setting met with two startling shocks during the summer of 1863, the first due to a fire that destroyed large portions of the town and the second due to its proximity to Gettysburg, just ten miles away. As a result, its residents experienced, firsthand, the ramp up to battle and all that brought with it—massive troop encampments, foraging soldiers and so on. And worse yet, they suffered through the dreadful aftermath of the battle, circumstances that saw hundreds of wounded cared for by many of its citizens, including the Daughters of Charity. Little did Kate Hewitt know that her fiancé's cruel fate, in neighboring Gettysburg on July 1, 1863, would lead her to Emmitsburg and the Daughters of Charity.[169]

True to the promise she made to John Reynolds, Kate Hewitt began the process of entering into a religious life in the year of his death. The fact that she had converted to Catholicism just two years prior (at Eden Hall) held her in good stead with the Catholic faith. One account indicates that a religious representative from Eden Hall applied to the Daughters of Charity in Emmitsburg, Maryland, on Kate's behalf just eight days after John Reynolds's funeral.[170]

It is intriguing to note that the Daughters of Charity admissions book indicates that Kate's residence at the time of acceptance was Huntington, New York. As discussed previously, this is interesting in and of itself because there appears to be no known association between Kate and Huntington, which is located on Long Island.[171]

Daughters of Charity archival records do confirm that Kate, before formally entering the Daughters of Charity, completed a period of "postulancy" at Mount Hope Retreat in Baltimore, Maryland. Per the Daughters of Charity, postulancy is a period of "formation" where a prospective sister experiences "living a spiritual, community and apostolic life in common"

S? JOSEPH'S ACADEMY NEAR EMMITSBURG M?

L. Enke's rendition of Saint Joseph's Academy and the surrounding countryside, circa 1860–70, provides an excellent depiction of the bucolic setting surrounding Emmitsburg, Maryland, at the time. *Library of Congress.*

while continuing to discern her vocation. At the time, Mount Hope was a private Catholic institution founded by the Sisters of Charity in 1840.[172]

After completing her postulancy, likely in either late February or early March 1864, Kate officially entered the Daughters of Charity. Her "vocation date," or date on which she entered St. Joseph's Seminary at the Daughters of Charity, was March 17, 1864. Per the Daughters of Charity, this stage of formation is called "the Seminary," and sisters at this stage are called "Seminary Sisters."[173]

Perhaps about the same time she officially entered the Daughters of Charity community, Kate received, as visitors, two of John Reynolds's sisters and his former orderly, Charles Veil. The group had just come from Gettysburg where Veil showed Reynolds's sisters the battlefield location where Reynolds was killed. Emmitsburg was a short ten miles from Gettysburg, and the group took advantage of the opportunity to visit Kate. During the visit, Kate gave Charles Veil a beautifully embroidered handkerchief she had originally intended to give Reynolds. Available

This rare 1867 view of St. Joseph's Academy and Daughters of Charity campus in Emmitsburg shows the scene as it appeared to Kate in 1864. *Courtesy of the Daughters of Charity Province of St. Louise, St. Louis, Missouri.*

sources indicate this visit likely took place in either the latter part of March or very early April 1864. More details on this encounter, and the handkerchief, appear in chapter 19.[174]

One of the few sources we have on Kate's years with the Daughters of Charity are the letters written by Ellie Reynolds to Charles Veil. These letters covered all sorts of subjects. But during the years 1865–68, Ellie typically included a few lines about Kate. Ellie usually offered comments relative to Kate's life with the Daughters of Charity, and she often referred to Kate's health.[175]

It seems Reynolds's family, especially Ellie, developed a deep bond with their brother's former orderly. It is easy to see why as Veil was with Reynolds the moment he was struck down by a Confederate bullet. Veil and two other staff officers were the first to move Reynolds off the battlefield. Veil was also among the group that accompanied Reynolds's body from Gettysburg (via Union Bridge, Westminster, and Baltimore, Maryland) to Philadelphia. And Veil conveyed the story of Reynolds's last moments to the family. Apparently, it was their visit to Emmitsburg to see Kate that inspired Ellie to regularly update Veil on Kate's status while also indicating to him Kate's interest in his welfare. It seems Kate, Ellie and Veil provided one another a tangible link to memories of John, both professional and personal.[176]

By October 2, 1864, Kate had finished her seminary and received the habit. At this time she also received her community name, Sister Hildegardis. Per a Daughters of Charity internet post about Kate, the Daughters of Charity assigned her this name. This conflicts with Reynolds family lore indicating Reynolds's sisters helped select Kate's community name. While

St. Joseph's Academy,
EMMITTSBURG, MD.

Kate would have attended services in this chapel. This 1890s image shows the chapel much as it would have looked during Kate's time with the Daughters of Charity in Emmitsburg. *Courtesy of the Daughters of Charity Province of St. Louise, St. Louis, Missouri.*

the information from the Daughters of Charity seems clear enough, there must be an explanation for this confusion. Unfortunately, no further information can be found to clear up this discrepancy. Perhaps, and this is only speculation, Kate was given the opportunity to pick her community name from a short list of names provided by the Daughters of Charity. In turn, maybe John's sisters helped Kate decide which name to select.[177]

During 1865, several letters from Ellie to Charles Veil provide a glimpse into Kate's life with the Daughters of Charity. A brief comment in a letter dated June 5, 1865—"Miss Hewitt writes in good spirts"—seems to imply that Kate was happy enough with her life as Sister Hildegardis. Then, in

August 1865, Ellie writes (to Veil), "Miss Hewitt sends you her kindest regards and says she is much pleased at your selection of active duty. Your late commander always having taken the active part." Regarding Kate's health, Ellie indicates, "She is very well & much happier looking than when you saw her—Her position is a settled one & she feels at home in her duties." And Ellie concludes her remarks about Kate by conveying to Veil, "On Saturday she was permitted to go alone with us to the mountains where we spent the morning. It was a very great pleasure to see so much of her & without other sisters being present."[178]

Then, in a letter written by Ellie to Charles Veil on October 9, 1865, Ellie offers the first indication that Kate had been experiencing significant issues with her health: "Miss Hewitt, now 'Sister Hildegardis' has been quite sick, since we left Emmitsburg but is well again." Regardless, at this point Kate had already begun to serve "missions" on behalf of the Daughters of Charity. Her first mission found her serving in the Emmitsburg community. This mission lasted just over a year (fall 1864 through early winter 1865). Finally, a letter written by Ellie to Veil on January 15, 1866, indicates Kate had left Emmitsburg to begin her second mission: "Miss Hewitt has gone to Albany & is teaching in a boys school there that the 'Sisters of Charity' recently opened. She passed thru Phila. in the night but stopped in Balt. for a few hours. Mrs. Gildersleve [*sic*] had the pleasure of seeing her there."[179]

Little did Kate (Sister Hildegardis) know what fate had in store for her at St. Joseph's School in Albany, New York. Suffice it to say, life wasn't through challenging Kate Hewitt's ability to adjust to change and overcome unexpected difficult circumstances. The question was, could she do it one more time?

17

KATE

THE DAUGHTERS OF CHARITY—ALBANY

She is not strong & has a cough that is almost constant.

Albany was not Emmitsburg. In fact, the difference between the two was like the difference between night and day. As the capital of New York, Albany was huge. It was home to a large population and multiple churches. Emmitsburg was a sleepy little country hamlet nestled in the foothills of the Catoctin Mountains. It was the home to the Daughters of Charity community. Yet for a sister of the Daughters of Charity, none of this likely mattered all that much, at least not initially. Irrespective of these differences in location, Kate Hewitt's concerns and responsibilities, as a sister, would be more or less the same. However, in Albany Kate found herself immersed in a vibrant and growing Catholic community. Seemingly, this might be a fitting place for Kate. In a matter of speaking, she had come "home," or at least back to her native state. What remained to be seen was whether or not her health would allow her to fulfill her commitment to the Daughters of Charity. Then too, would the Daughters of Charity community continue to fulfill their commitment to Kate? In short, when the five-year trial period of her service to the Daughters of Charity community came, would Kate make her vows? As Kate arrived in Albany during the winter of 1866, there was certainly much to consider, not the least of which was coming to know her new home.

The first St. Joseph's Church in Albany, New York, was dedicated on May 7, 1843. St Joseph's was the third Catholic church in the city at that time,

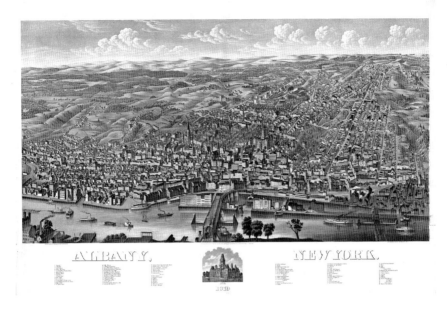

ALBANY, NEW YORK.

This bird's-eye view of Albany shows the capital city much like it appeared during Kate Hewitt's time as a resident of the city. *Library of Congress.*

and it was built to accommodate the growing Catholic community north of the downtown area. It was located at the northeast corner of North Pearl and Lumber Streets. This section of town was called the "Lumber District" of Albany due to the large amount of lumber passing through the nearby docks. By 1846, per George Rogers Howell's and Jonathan Tenney's *History of Albany*, "The parish made rapid progress," and as a result it was not long before yet another new building on North Pearl was established as a "Girl's Orphan Asylum." Following this, schools were established for "both boys and girls" and a "handsome" parochial residence was built. The orphanage was named St. Vincent's Orphan Asylum.[180]

Soon enough, the fast-growing St. Joseph's parish necessitated a new church. Designed by "celebrated architect" Patrick Keeley, who also designed Albany's Cathedral of the Immaculate Conception, the new St. Joseph's Church was dedicated in May 1860. Standing on a lot bounded by Ten Broeck, Second and First Streets (also known as Ten Broeck Triangle), the stunning edifice featured medieval architecture and stood 212 feet high and 116 feet wide. The remarkable church boasted three marble altars and beautiful stained-glass windows detailing "nearly all the principal events in the life of the Redeemer."[181]

ST. JOSEPHS CATHOLIC CHURCH
ALBANY, N.Y.
VERY REV. THOMAS M. A. BURKE, PASTOR. A.D.1871.

This image shows an artist's rendition of Albany's St. Joseph's Church much as it would have appeared at the time of Kate Hewitt's arrival in Albany. In actuality, the forward steeple was not complete when the church opened its doors but was completed some years later. *Library of Congress.*

With the coming of the new church, the old church on the northeast corner of North Pearl and Lumber was converted to a boys school. While teaching at St. Joseph's in the 1860s, sisters of the Daughters of Charity lived at 261 North Pearl Street. Their residence and the school were located in the same building that had originally housed St. Vincent's Orphanage. St. Vincent's moved out of the building in 1865 and moved to a location in the Lumber District at the corner of North Ferry Street and Broadway. When the orphanage was relocated in 1865, almost all the orphans were transferred to the new location.[182]

When Kate Hewitt (Sister Hildegardis) arrived in Albany, only twelve students remained at the school, and that became the beginnings of St. Joseph's Industrial School, which was established on August 19, 1865. When Kate Hewitt began her tenure at St. Joseph's School, Sister Helen Ryan was the "Sister Servant," or in other words, she was the sister in charge at the school. Interestingly, Sister Helen was one and the same "Catherine Ryan" who would later become Kate Hewitt's partner in running a Select School (private school) of their own.[183]

During Kate's mission in Albany, the only window we have into her personal feelings about her situation and her health are letters Ellie Reynolds sent to Charles Veil. In August 1866, Ellie conveys to Veil that "Miss Hewitt is very well now & is stationed at Albany teaching in one of their schools. She has not been well during the winter—I hope to go on and see her in a few weeks." She continued, "Her [Kate's] letters are few and short but she always asks for you & desires to be kindly remembered." In a letter written just a few days later, Ellie indicated that "we [Reynolds's sisters] expect to visit her at Albany in the fall."[184]

Ellie made good on her intentions to visit Kate as she detailed in a letter to Veil, written on January 15, 1867, "Miss Hewitt is very well, we spent a week with her at Albany, (I do not think I have written you since), in October

This building, located at 261 North Pearl Street, once housed the sisters of the Daughters of Charity. In 1865, it became St. Joseph's School, where Sister Hildegardis (Kate Hewitt) taught. *Courtesy of the Daughters of Charity Province of St. Louise, St. Louis, Missouri.*

and cheered her somewhat. She expects [us] to make her [Kate] a yearly visit and we long to do so. I do not know which of us enjoyed it more. She asks for you in all our letters (which I am sorry to say are not as frequent as I would wish) and would write you if she were allowed."[185]

But six months later, it seems as though Kate's health took a turn for the worse. On August 11, 1868, Ellie wrote, "Miss Hewitt is still at Albany. I hope we shall visit her in October. *She is not* [*strong*] *& has a cough that is almost constant*" (emphasis added). Little did Ellie know that not only had Kate's health taken a turn for the worse, but also, apparently, so had her status within the Daughters of Charity community.[186]

A few things are worth noting before unfolding the story of Kate's demise with the Daughters of Charity. It is clear from reading these letters that aside from Ellie writing to Veil, Kate had been writing to Ellie, though perhaps not as often and voluminously as Ellie would have preferred. Sadly, the letters Kate sent to Ellie appear not to have survived. Also, one thing seems to resonate in Ellie's correspondence with Charles Veil—Kate was struggling periodically with her health. In fact, it seems she had developed a serious issue with a chronic cough by August 1868. Thus, it appears that the cough that is described by Ellie as "almost constant" in August 1868 may very likely have been a manifestation of consumption (tuberculosis). Finally, Ellie's letters to Veil offer a small bit of insight into Kate's state of mind with regard to her new life with the Daughters of Charity. In the August 1868 letter, Ellie mentions that Kate "is happier as a 'sister'" than she could be "in the world." This statement seems to offer an indication that Kate would likely make her vows and commit to spending the remaining years of her life as a member of the Daughters of Charity community. Time would tell in this regard, for it seems that once again the unexpected forces of fate would combine to shape her future in an unanticipated fashion.[187]

In 2005, Marian Latimer's monograph *Is She Kate?* revealed a shocking story. As it happens, there is a note in the records of the Daughters of Charity archives from an August 1868 Council meeting at the St. Joseph's Industrial School pertaining to Kate Hewitt's exit from the school. The note states, "The council is of the opinion that Sister Hewitt of the St. Joseph's School, had better return to her friends—being of a very violent temper, they do not think she is called to our state of life." This seems to be a complete turnaround from how the sisters at Eden Hall felt about Kate and is, in fact, the only known primary source of this nature. Be that as it may, this note *appears* to reveal the reason Kate left the Daughters of Charity. That said, one is left to wonder if there is more to the story. Regardless, whether she left voluntarily or not, Kate abruptly left the Daughters of Charity community on September 3, 1868.[188]

By September 1868, it had been a little over five years since John Reynolds's death. Kate Hewitt had spent four and a half of those years as a member of the Daughters of Charity. And for all intents and purposes, it appeared she had found a home. But despite her dedicated service to the religious community, she, once again, found herself starting over. On a grander scale, Kate's life had seemingly taken another life-altering turn. Indeed, this would not be the last twist of fate in Kate's tumultuous life.

One other fact is worth of mentioning. Though Ellie Reynolds continued to write to Charles Veil through 1901, she never again mentioned Kate after her letter of August 1868. It can only be surmised that the fact that Kate left the Daughters of Charity community changed Ellie's feelings toward Kate. Of course, it is also possible Kate ceased communication with Ellie. Unfortunately, no primary source documents are available to shed light on this subject. Having said all this, it does seem odd that Ellie, the diligent archivist of letters she received from Reynolds family members as well as others, would not have saved the letters she received from Kate—that is, unless something affected her to the point where she cared not to preserve these letters for posterity. Was it Kate's leaving the Daughters of Charity? Or was there more? Perhaps it was not only the fact that Kate left the religious community, but also what happened next in Kate's life.

18

KATE

MARRIAGE

A nuptial mass was celebrated…

By the fall of 1868, Kate Hewitt had packed a lot of living in her thirty-two years. None of it had been easy. Left to fend for herself early in life, she mysteriously fell into a life of prostitution. Despite ending up on the "wrong side of the tracks," she began to right the wrongs in her personal life by embracing the Catholic faith. And with this change came a newfound love and a commitment to marry. But as we have seen, this only led to calamity, as she lost her fiancé, General John Reynolds, in the most tragic of circumstances. Then, after giving her life to God as Sister Hildegardis of the Daughters of Charity community, she began to suffer a menacing cough and unrelenting illness. After four and a half years, it seemed she had found a home with the Daughters of Charity and was actually about to make her vows, thereby signifying her everlasting commitment to her religious community. But just before doing so, she curiously found herself ostracized from the religious community in which she had sought refuge. Finally, after all of this, she was, once again, left to fend for herself. A person of less fortitude would likely have given up, but not Kate. Courageously, she would see things through, one way or another. Yet in attempting to do so, Kate Hewitt would need all the perseverance and strength she could muster. Kate had lived in Albany as a sister with the Daughters of Charity community for a few years, but she had been in a group environment and her exposure to the outside world had been very limited. This would be different. Now, she was on her own.

This rare image taken from the west side of Albany's North Pearl Street captured the row of buildings that included the property purchased by Kate Hewitt after she left the Daughters of Charity Community. The third building in the row from the left, 103 North Pearl, was Kate's residence and, for a brief time, the location of her "Select School." *Courtesy of Albany Public Library.*

The capital of the great state of New York was home to everything typically found in a large city of that time. Boasting a population of nearly seventy thousand by 1870, Albany was then the twentieth-largest city in the United States. Numerous ethnic groups called the city home, with the Irish, German and Jewish leading the way. The city served not only as the state seat of government but also as a major transportation and trade hub both for seaborne and land travel, most notably the Erie Canal, gateway to America's heartland. Home to numerous banks, large hotels and prominent newspapers, among other things, the city featured plenty of hustle and bustle. Like San Francisco, Albany also came with all the dangerous trappings of any big city. The potential for danger, misfortune and bad choices, especially for a single woman in mid-nineteenth-century America, lurked around every corner. But Kate Hewitt was not your typical single woman. Certainly, her life experiences held her in good stead, as she was wise beyond her years. Kate was smart, and she was savvy. And she would not "backslide." Instead, she would find her niche in the burgeoning Albany community, and she would be quite successful in doing so.[189]

It did not take Kate Hewitt long to bounce back. By November 1868, she had purchased a property, at 103 North Pearl Street. And in December of the same year, an advertisement ran in a local paper highlighting the opening of "Miss Hewitt's Select School" (located in Albany). Today, this would be called a private school. It seems Kate's efforts as an independent teacher proved successful; within a year, Kate joined with the aforementioned Catherine Ryan in operating the school, which was located at 81 North Pearl Street. It is worth noting that this address places the school in one of the city's most historic buildings, the Lansing-Pemberton building. Also known as "Pemberton Corner," this building no longer stands. Regarding the partnership of Hewitt and Ryan, Kate's business partner was indeed the same Catherine Ryan who was also a former Sister of the Daughters of Charity community. (Ryan left the community six months after Kate, in March 1869.) Kate and Catherine operated the school together for a few years and also, for a time, co-owned Kate's nearby property at 103 North Pearl Street. But by the summer of 1871, they had dissolved their partnership, and Kate also bought out Catherine's share of ownership in the property they had co-owned at 103 North Pearl. Both Kate and Catherine continued to teach after that time, but independently and at different locations, with Kate teaching for one more year (1872–73) at 81 North Pearl and then at her 103 North Pearl residence (1873–74).[190]

It is fascinating that even though Kate left the Daughters of Charity community under less than ideal circumstances, it seems her heart never strayed far from her faith. One example of her ongoing commitment to her religion came in December 1872, when Kate gave a benefit "entertainment" event at

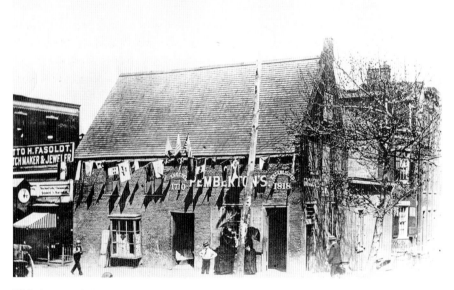

This image of Albany's famed Lansing House at "Pemberton's Corner" shows the location as it very likely appeared during the time Kate Hewitt and Catherine Ryan operated their "Select School" in some portion of this multilevel structure. Though the sheer odds are against it, the two women standing by the building are intriguing in that the nearby presence of the well-dressed young boy points to the possibility that he was a student and the two women were Kate and Catherine. *Courtesy of Albany Public Library.*

This family Bible was given to Joseph and Catherine (Kate) on the occasion of their marriage by Joseph's brother Gervas P.A. Pfordt. *Courtesy of Liz Anibal Werner.*

her home (such events typically featured student musical performances, crafts and so forth). Funds raised from this event were donated to the Little Sisters of the Poor. Regardless, by the summer of 1874 change was definitely "in the air" for Kate Hewitt. In June of that year, Kate's school held the last year-end exhibition it would ever hold. But why? Had Kate's struggle with consumption (tuberculosis) gotten the best of her? Was she no longer able to teach? Or was there something else? There seems to be no doubt that Kate continued to suffer significantly with her health. Nevertheless, it appears there was indeed something else or, more accurately, *someone* else.[191]

The next turn of events in Kate's life revolved around an Albany florist named Joseph Pfordt. Pfordt's family business often brought him in to contact with St. Joseph's Church for weddings, funerals and other events. As a result, it appears Kate had likely come to know Joseph during her tenure with the Daughters of Charity community. Apparently, Kate and Joseph became acquainted on a much more personal basis once Kate left the Daughters of Charity. Unfortunately, no letters or documents survive to shed light on how their relationship progressed from mere acquaintance to a couple falling in love and courtship. Thankfully, the Pfordt family Bible provides a few key pieces of information pertaining to the result of their growing love for each other.

ST. JOSEPH'S CHURCH, ALBANY, N. Y.

This view from the balcony shows the interior of Albany's St. Joseph's Church in all its glory. Note the ornate altar where Joseph and Catherine (Kate) were married. *Author's collection.*

Per an Albany newspaper marriage announcement, church records and the Pfordt family Bible, on June 24, 1874, a nuptial mass held at St. Joseph's Church in Albany celebrated the joining together of Catherine Mary Hewitt and Joseph B. Pfordt as husband and wife. With this, it appears the woman who had once loved and been engaged to General John Reynolds, only to lose him so tragically, once again found happiness. Evidence also indicates that Kate's marriage was welcomed by Joseph's family, as Joseph's brother Gervais was the individual who gave Kate and Joseph the family Bible as a wedding gift. Such a gift would not have been given without careful consideration and deep affection.[192]

Unfortunately, little is known about Kate's life with Joseph. We do know that Joseph and Kate lived at 897 Broadway Street (above the family florist shop). The greenhouse was located next door, at 899 Broadway. Though information on Kate's marriage is sparse, quite a bit of information pertaining to one important facet of Kate's life appears in numerous newspapers of the time—not only Albany newspapers but also papers far and wide. Fortunately, these articles provide great detail on one significant aspect of Kate's life that added to her legacy.[193]

19

KATE

A REMARKABLE LEGACY

*One time fiancée of John Reynolds, devout Christian woman,
inspiring teacher, award winning artist, and dedicated wife.*

By the twilight of her life, Kate Hewitt had shown herself to be a
survivor. Once an orphan who found troubled waters, she sought
refuge in religious conversion. Finding love with a dashing soldier, her
hopes of marriage were all too soon dashed by his tragic death at Gettysburg.
As a result, she gave her life to God. But when her plans for a cloistered life
went awry, she found refuge in teaching. And finally she found love again. All
the while she suffered with a menacing disease. Yet somehow Kate Hewitt
persevered. In considering all of this, it seems Kate's legacy was complete.
However, there was one more aspect of her life yet to come to the fore.

One thing that seems to have endured throughout Kate's life was her
love of embroidery. As stated earlier, she was described as "well educated,"
and we can assume that she learned her embroidery skills during her
early education. As stated in an article titled "Stitching It Together," most
embroidery skills at that time were learned "at private academies, often quite
expensive boarding or day schools, under the watchful eye of the female
instructor who guided the layout and design and taught the various stitches."
Regardless of where and how she learned to embroider, by the time Kate
was an adult she had acquired what was described by one source as *"great
taste in design and workmanship, displaying extraordinary skill"* in embroidery (italics
added for emphasis).[194]

Interestingly, the first mention of Kate's needle skills is from John Reynolds's orderly, Charles Veil. As detailed previously, after Reynolds's death, two of his sisters, along with Reynolds's former orderly, visited Kate Hewitt at St. Joseph's Seminary in Emmitsburg, Maryland. It was during this visit that Kate presented Veil with a beautifully embroidered handkerchief she had been preparing for John, prior to his death. Veil later related the experience as follows:

> *Taking from the folds of her dress a small package, she handed it to me. I thanked her for it and we left. After we had left the convent I told the sisters of what had taken place and, on opening the little package which was nicely done up and tied with a ribbon, found a very beautiful embroidered handkerchief—the coat of arms of the United States, very beautifully done. I have the handkerchief and token to this day.*[195]

Ultimately, Kate made quite a name for herself with this talent. Initially, her embroidery talents were recognized locally. In 1871, an article in the *Albany Evening Journal* describes an exhibition of household items at the "Domestic Hall." The article details an exhibit "by Mrs. C.M. Hewitt of this city" that consisted of "satin stole, silk cushions and flannel skirt, richly embroidered with silk twist and bullion." It was said that her exhibit "attracts the attention of every passer." Another article in the *Daily Albany Argus* details the same exhibit, indicating that Kate's pieces "exhibit much genius while the execution is faultless." It also says that "the lady teaches the art," alluding to the fact that Kate, among other things, taught embroidery at her "Select School."[196]

Then, in July 1875, an article in the *Daily Albany Argus* provided details on a large "Elegant Banner" that was commissioned for the St. Jean Baptiste Society. It was a banner of heavy white silk and was seven feet high by five feet wide. The banner was designed by a Mr. E.P. Treadwell of Albany. The article went on to share that the embroidery work, which included "various tints of silk and twist," was done by "Mrs. Joseph Pfordt." It was said to be "a credit to her excellent taste and skill." The article also stated that "Mrs. Pfordt has a keen appreciation of the beautiful in nature and art, which she has clearly shown in the completion of the elegant banner."[197]

Within a year, Kate's amazing talent had found a proper forum, albeit far from her home. Its formal name seemed a bit stilted, the International Exhibition of Arts, Manufactures, and Products and Soil and Mine. Fortunately its colloquial name stuck, "The Centennial Exhibition." The

Left: This rare Mathew Brady photo of Lieutenant Charles Veil was owned for years by his great-grandnephew, Fred W. Veil. Fred, former director of the Sharlot Hall Museum in Prescott, Arizona, donated this image to the museum, and thanks to Fred's stewardship it is now preserved for perpetuity. *Courtesy of Sharlot Hall Museum Library & Archives. Charles Veil Papers, Call Number 215.00089.001.*

Below: Another rare image once owned by Fred W. Veil, this extraordinary and seldom published image shows the handkerchief Kate Hewitt had been preparing for John Reynolds just prior to his untimely death. The artistry evident in the handkerchief clearly demonstrates Kate's remarkable embroidery skills. *Courtesy of Sharlot Hall Museum (ACC# 215.089).*

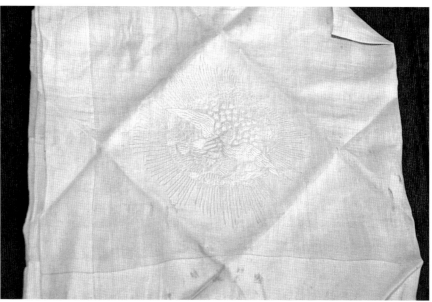

event celebrated a special anniversary, the centennial of the signing of the Declaration of Independence. Sprawled over 236 acres in Philadelphia's Fairmount Park, the fair marked the first in the country to rise to national and international prominence. Thirty-six countries were represented, and over its six-month run nearly ten million individuals attended the exhibition. As Kimberly Orcutt so astutely observed in her remarkable book, *Power and Prosperity, American Art at Philadelphia's 1876 Centennial Exhibition*, that represented nearly one-fourth of the entire U.S. population.[198]

As it happened, Kate was commissioned to create a special banner representing New York for the Centennial Exhibition. And true to form, her remarkable skills shone brightly as her banner drew praises not only from the local Albany press but also from newspapers far and wide, to include prominent papers such as the *Chicago Tribune*. In fact, the *Tribune* columnist indicated that "there are two remarkable works on exhibition [in] the Women's Pavilion" and commented, "In the presence of these works, one is overcome rather with awe than with admiration." The columnist continued to extol Kate's fine art as follows:

> *One is a banner nearly 6 feet square. The material is white satin, and upon this ground is wrought the most delicate and ingenious embroidery that I ever saw. There is fringe around the silk, tastefully and elaborately designed. In the centre is a representation of the Great Seal of the United States, so faithfully worked out as to convey the perfect impression of a fine painting. Of course it is in many colors, yet all rich and harmonious. One side of the banner shows the coat-of-arms, the double eagle, and the shield, with the eternally grand motto, "E Pluribus Unum"; while underneath are twin sprigs of oak, leaved and adorned, forming a graceful half-wreath. The opposite side shows the Pyramid rising out of the desert. Nothing could be more perfect, as a work of art.*[199]

According to the *Albany Evening Journal*, Kate paid for the supplies for this banner, and in order to earn back some of the money, the banner was put up for sale at the close of the exhibition. At that time, it was valued at $2,000; today this would be nearly $50,000.[200]

Interestingly, though the Women's Pavilion was not one of the five main buildings at the Philadelphia International Exhibition, it was the first of its kind at an international exposition. Funds to erect the thirty-thousand-square-foot wooden building were raised exclusively by the Women's Committee, and the pavilion included, among other things, art, engineering,

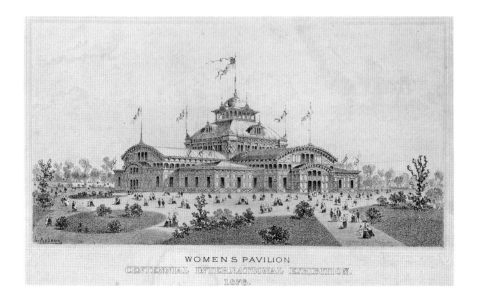

WOMENS PAVILION
CENTENNIAL INTERNATIONAL EXHIBITION.
1876.

religion and fashion. The focus on women's exhibits represented quite an achievement, as never before had as many exhibits created by women, as compared to total exhibits, occurred at a world's fair.[201]

In reflecting on Kate's artwork, it seems she had come full circle with her embroidery work, from talented student, to teacher of the craft and finally to award-winning artist as her banner earned special recognition at the Centennial Exhibition. It is worth noting here that embroidery accomplished at the artistic level demonstrated by Kate takes more than talent, it takes patience, it takes dedication, it takes determination and it takes perseverance. Fittingly, these were qualities Kate demonstrated throughout her life as she faced seemingly endless challenges. Moreover, all of this seems quite ironic when one considers the fact that Kate's banner hung in a special women's pavilion in the same city where she had once come to begin her life anew, at Eden Hall. And this was also the same city in which she had viewed her former fiancé's remains after his untimely death at Gettysburg.[202]

Sadly, Kate's centennial banner would serve as her last mark in life. On Friday, October 6, 1876, after only two years of marriage, Catherine "Kate" Mary Hewitt Pfordt died at her home in Albany, New York. The cause of death, not surprisingly, was listed as consumption. This seems to dovetail with the fact that John Reynolds's sisters had noted Kate's continual struggles with her health, dating from the mid-1860s, especially a persistent cough. Kate's duties as a postulant and as a sister likely placed her in contact with many ill individuals. Regardless, Kate somehow

Opposite: The Women's Pavilion was among the most ornate of the buildings constructed for the Philadelphia Centennial Exhibition. One of the most written about and highly praised items on display in this building was Kate (Hewitt) Pfordt's banner. *Library of Congress.*

Above: This unique view shows the inside of the Women's Pavilion. Unfortunately, no extant photos show Kate (Hewitt) Pfordt's prize-winning banner (the banner in this image is not Kate's). *Library of Congress.*

endured the pain and suffering of the awful disease long enough to serve her faith admirably and ultimately to once again find love.[203]

Kate's funeral took place at the Sacred Heart Church in Albany on Sunday, October 8, 1876. The eulogy was delivered by pastor Father Maguire. No records survive with regard to who might have attended Kate's funeral, but one obituary indicates it was "very largely attended." Certainly Joseph and his family would have been there. Interestingly, an Owego, New York newspaper report published a few weeks after Kate's funeral detailed one Benjamin Hewitt's return to Owego, New York, after traveling to Albany for his sister Kate's funeral. This seems to be an indication that, whatever the cause of the original estrangement between Kate and Benjamin, they had likely reconciled. Another clue that Kate and Benjamin had made amends was the fact that Kate left some property to Benjamin in her will. Aside from all of this, there is one final interesting note pertaining to Kate's demise; she is buried at St. Agnes Cemetery, Menards, New York, the very cemetery known to be the final resting place for most of the sisters from Albany's Daughters of Charity community.[204]

One obituary described Kate as a "true Christian woman" while also indicating "at one point of her life this estimable lady was a cloistered nun in the Roman Catholic Sisterhood." Another obituary stated that she was "a lady of high abilities, an earnest and consistent Christian and was well known and highly respected." Father Maguire echoed these

The Philadelphia Centennial Exhibition Medal, face and reverse side. Kate (Hewitt) Pfordt received this award for the remarkably embroidered banner she created for the event. *Internet Archive Book Images (via flickr), George E. Marks,* A Treatise on Marks' Patent Artificial Limbs with Rubber Hands and Feet *(New York, A.A. Marks, c1888), 140.*

statements while celebrating the funeral mass, as he mentioned that Kate was "an earnest Christian lady and a benefactor of every good cause." One can only hope that Kate's faith and her years with Joseph, though far too few, provided times of joy and happiness that offset her struggle with consumption and her ongoing battle to rise above the trials life presented to her throughout her life.[205]

Finally, fate would bestow one final bittersweet twist in Kate's story. On the very day Kate died, news was received that the spectacular banner she had created for the Philadelphia Centennial Exhibition was selected for an award for its remarkable artistry in embroidery. One is left to wonder if she knew. Regardless, in the end, Kate Hewitt's legacy endures. Indeed, she made her mark in life in many ways. She was a woman of strength and perseverance and a talented teacher who positively influenced innumerable lives. She was a Catholic convert and devout Christian lady who, having seen the light of God, never lost her faith. She was an award-winning embroiderer and the loving wife of Joseph B. Pfordt. And last, but certainly not least, Catherine "Kate" Mary Hewitt Pfordt was the one-time fiancée of General John Fulton Reynolds.[206]

20

JOHN AND KATE

REFLECTIONS

What they did here.

Gettysburg's Lost Love Story: The Ill-Fated Romance of General John Reynolds and Kate Hewitt is a story with many twists and turns of fate. Kate's and John's backgrounds could not have been more different; one was an orphan, the other a child of privilege. Then again, as we all know, love knows no bounds. While Reynolds learned to adhere to the strict discipline of an officer in the U.S. Army, Kate found herself lost in a sordid world as she did what she felt necessary to support herself and an adopted sister. Yet fate brought these two unsuspecting individuals together. At forty, John Reynolds was not getting any younger, and though a confirmed bachelor, he was a family man who must have yearned for a soul mate. And Kate, escaping a colorful past to embark on a new beginning, likely never expected to meet the love of her life as her sojourn began. Nevertheless, they did meet and they fell deeply in love.

Sadly, just three short years after falling in love and committing their lives to each other, Reynolds was killed at Gettysburg. Though she had become accustomed to dealing with some of the harshest realities of life, the loss of John transcended everything in Kate's life. Even so, somehow, she found a way to survive. At that point in her life, she was only twenty-seven years old. But she had experienced all that life had to offer—the good, the bad and everything in between. She knew the loneliness that only an orphan could know. She had endured life on the wrong side of the tracks, both as a prostitute and as the central figure in a scandalous affair. But despite all of this, she escaped her past through a religious awakening and conversion to Catholicism. And along the way, she also found true love. Unfortunately, this love came with a tragic twist. This calamity led Kate to seek refuge in her faith.

Finally, Kate's fate came with one more unexpected turn, a change from her commitment to her faith, as a member of a religious community, to a commitment to a newfound love and marriage. In the end, the illness that had haunted her for at least a decade dashed her hopes for a long life as a wife to Joseph Pfordt and mother to his children. The word that seems to apply best to Kate Hewitt's life is *perseverance*. Time and again she was faced with seemingly insurmountable personal challenges. But somehow, like a boxer repeatedly knocked to the canvas, she found a way to pick herself up off the mat. In the end, this much is certain; at forty years of age, her life was much too short. But the spirit and determination shown by Kate Hewitt, often against terrific odds, offer all of us a lesson we can take to heart.

John Reynolds died at age forty-two, thus he experienced two more years of life than Kate. His story has been well known since his time—soldier, patriot and martyred war hero. His legacy is set in stone, both literally and figuratively. In point of fact, there is no mistaking where he was in action and where he was when killed at Gettysburg, as monuments and markers clearly indicate these locations. Beautifully sculpted portrait statues of Reynolds also memorialize him at Gettysburg, one in the Soldiers National Cemetery and one on the Pennsylvania state monument. Perhaps more importantly, Reynolds was revered in his own time. Fittingly, a soldier likely said it best, "His death at the time affected us much, for he was one of the soldier Generals of the army, a man whose soul was in his country's work, which he did with a soldier's high honor and fidelity."[207]

Until now, Kate's story and legacy has not been so well known. Though portions of Kate's story had been told, the details of her California years remained undiscovered. And her ultimate fate after leaving the Daughters of Charity remained a mystery for over 150 years. Hopefully this account has brought the collective stories of John Reynolds and Kate Hewitt to life in a fashion that allows for a fuller understanding of their ill-fated romance. In the end, though this story is wrought with misfortune and heartbreak, it is one of triumph as well in the form of Kate's perseverance.

Sadly, the location of Kate Hewitt's grave remained a mystery to students of history for over a century and a half. In fact, the specific location of her grave was known only to her husband, Joseph, and his

The remarkable equestrian monument of General Reynolds and his trusted steed is the work of celebrated sculptor Henry Kirke Bush-Brown. Dedicated on July 1, 1899, the monument weighs some nine thousand pounds, and amazingly, only two hoofs balance Reynolds and the horse on the pedestal. Reynolds always loved horses and was a splendid horseman, thus it is fitting that he and his horse overlook, for eternity, the hallowed ground at Gettysburg that he opted to defend on the morning of July 1, 1863.[208] *Courtesy of Archives and Special Collections, Franklin and Marshall College, Lancaster, Pennsylvania.*

Left: This marker, dedicated on July 1, 1886, identifies the site where General Reynolds fell on July 1, 1863. Reynolds's orderly Charles Veil showed members of the Reynolds family where General Reynolds was killed. *Loski collection.*

Right: This truly unique engraving of the General John F. Reynolds memorial located in the Soldiers National Cemetery at Gettysburg appeared in *Frank Leslie's Popular Monthly*, August 1888. The Reynolds statue was the first portrait statue on the battlefield and is the work of sculptor John Quincy Adams Ward. *Boardman Collection.*

family and then only until their passing. Fortunately, recent research conducted by the aforementioned genealogist Mary Stanford Pitkin and this author led us to the location of Kate's final resting place. And though Kate had rested in anonymity in the Pfordt family lot at Albany's St. Agnes Cemetery, under a shared stone representing numerous family members, the cemetery interment book confirms she does rest in the Pfordt family lot at Saint Agnes. But true to form, Kate has left us with one lasting mystery. Though she rests in the Pfordt family lot, the exact grave she rests in, within the family lot, remains uncertain. (The original interment book did not include such detail.) Be that as it may, in June 2021, a gravestone was placed in the family lot "in memoriam" of Kate. Fittingly, at long last, Kate has her "memorial."

Rest in peace John Fulton Reynolds and Catherine "Kate" Mary Hewitt Pfordt, your lives continue to have meaning all these years later. Those who

Left: This statue of John Reynolds appears as part of the Pennsylvania state monument at Gettysburg and is the work of sculptor Lee Lawrie. *Boardman Collection.*

Below: The obelisk in the family plot at Lancaster Cemetery marks General John Reynolds's grave. Note the crossed artillery tubes with the number three indicating Reynolds' association with the Third U.S. Artillery. William Reynolds, U.S. Navy admiral, is buried next to General Reynolds (to the right in this photo, note the anchor on the top of the mausoleum). *Courtesy of Lancaster History, Lancaster, Pennsylvania.*

This page: Catherine Hewitt Pfordt's new gravestone (located at the foot of the large preexisting Pfordt family stone) in the Pfordt family lot at St. Agnes Cemetery, Menands, New York. *Courtesy of Christopher S. White, Albany Grave Digger Genealogical Services & Cemetery Conservation.*

have lost loved ones on the field of battle, especially the parents, spouses, would-be future spouses, children and loved ones, face many challenges. Often these challenges represent seemingly insurmountable obstacles. Sadly, some prove unable to come to grips with such grievous losses. Somehow Kate Hewitt, though staggered by her loss, did not falter. Despite losing John and all the cruel blows life had dealt her, somehow she managed to stay the course. Hopefully, she was proud of herself for doing so. She should have been. Certainly John would have been proud of her. Perhaps having learned of her story, you are too.

Regardless, the wish and hope here is that this work will help you better remember the heroism, tragedy and sacrifice that took place at Gettysburg and the impact all of this had on countless firesides all across the nation. And hopefully, you will never forget, in the words of President Abraham Lincoln, "what they did here."

NOTES

Epigraph

1. Henry J. Hunt, "The First Day at Gettysburg," in Robert Underwood Johnson and Clarence Clough Buel, eds., *Battles and Leaders of the Civil War*, 4 vols. (1880–1884; repr., Edison, NJ: Castle Books, 1995), vol. 3, 277. According to *Battles and Leaders*, Hunt derived this quote from the famous quote regarding the heroism of Colonel Ridge as detailed in the "Assault of Badajos" in William Francis Patrick Napier's *History of the War in the Peninsula and in the South of France: From the Year 1807 to the Year 1814* (multiple printings, for details see Oxford, OH: David Christy, 1838), 448. Interestingly, Confederate general Henry Heth, per his memoirs (edited by James Morrison), made the same observation regarding General Lewis Armistead, who died leading his brigade during Longstreet's Assault (Pickett's Charge) at Gettysburg.

Preface

2. Thomas A. Desjardin, *These Honored Dead, How the Story of Gettysburg Shaped American Memory* (Cambridge, MA: Da Capo Press, 2003), 7.

Acknowledgements

3. Mary Hopkin's 1968 single "Those Were the Days," produced by Paul McCartney.

1. John: Gettysburg

4. E.M. Woodward, *History of the Third Pennsylvania Reserve* (Trenton, NJ: MacCrellish & Quigley, 1883), 159; Edward J. Nichols, *Toward Gettysburg: A Biography of General John F. Reynolds* (University Park: Pennsylvania State University Press, 1958), 113; Michael A. Riley, *"For God's Sake, Forward": General John F. Reynolds USA* (Gettysburg, PA: Farnsworth House Military Impressions, 1995), 32.

5. Diana Loski, "'For the Country's Sake': John Reynolds at Gettysburg," *The Gettysburg Experience*, April 2020, 40; Riley, *For God's Sake*, 35; Frank Aretas Haskell, *The Battle of Gettysburg* (Madison, Wisconsin History Commission, 1908), 14; Frederick L. Hitchcock, *War from the Inside* (Philadelphia: J.B. Lippincott, 1904), 101–2.

6. Dr. Jon M. Nese, PhD, and Jeff Harding, "Pickett's Charge—'A Perfect Storm of Heat,'" unpublished manuscript (scheduled to be published July 2022, in *Gettysburg Magazine*); Stephen Minot Weld, *War Diary and Letters of Stephen Minot Weld, 1861–1865* (Cambridge, MA: Riverside Press, 1912), 229. The modern-day average high in early July is around eighty-five degrees. Jacobs recorded temperatures at 7;00 a.m., 2:00 p.m. and 9:00 p.m. The highest temperature he recorded for the day was seventy-six at 2:00 p.m. The actual high may have been a few degrees higher if one allows for the so-called heat lag effect.

7. Edwin B. Coddington, *The Gettysburg Campaign, A Study in Command* (New York: Charles Scribner's Sons, 1968), 122, 238, 262; Nichols, *Toward Gettysburg*, 200; Riley, *For God's Sake*, 47.

8. Coddington, *Gettysburg Campaign*, 262–63, 682n14.

9. Coddington, *Gettysburg Campaign*, 689n79; Nichols, *Toward Gettysburg*, 202; Riley *For God's Sake*, 47–48; John W. Busey and David G. Martin, *Regimental Strengths and Losses at Gettysburg* (Highstown, NJ: Longstreet House, 1982), 101–2 and 172–84.

10. Coddington, *Gettysburg Campaign*, 267; Nichols, *Toward Gettysburg*, 202; Riley, *For God's Sake*, 48–49; Scott D. Hartwig, "At Great Risk," *America's Civil War* 32, no. 4 (September 2019): 12–13.

11. Coddington, *Gettysburg Campaign*, 267–68; Nichols, *Toward Gettysburg*, 203–4; Riley, *Toward Gettysburg*, 48–49.

12. John Reynolds Participant Account File, Gettysburg National Military Park, transcribed letter, Charles Veil to David McConaughy, April 7, 1864 [hereafter GNMP Veil–McConaughy letter], for copy of original see Charles H. Veil to David McConaughy, April 7, 1864, David McConaughy Papers, MS-022, Special Collections, Musselman Library, Gettysburg College; Loski, "For the Country's Sake," 43.

13. GNMP Veil–McConaughy letter (the Reynolds quote is listed exactly as it was written in Veil's letter); Reynolds Family Papers, MS 06, Series X, John Fulton Reynolds [hereafter Reynolds Family Papers], William Riddle to Lt. Bouvier, August 4, 1863; Nichols, *Toward Gettysburg*, 204–5; Coddington, *Gettysburg Campaign*, 268–69; *Riley, For God's Sake*, 49–51.
14. GNMP Veil–McConaughy letter; Nichols, *Toward Gettysburg*, 205–7; Coddington, *Gettysburg Campaign*, 686–687n52; Riley, *For God's Sake*, 51–52; Harry W. Pfanz, *Gettysburg—The First Day* (Chapel Hill: University of North Carolina Press, 2001), 77–79; Kalina Ingham Hintz, "When the General Fell: The Monumental Death of John F. Reynolds," *Blue and Gray Magazine* 22, no. 2 (Spring 2005): 24–28.
15. Reynolds Family Papers, William Riddle to Eleanor Reynolds, August 6, 1863.

2. John: Child of Privilege

16. Joseph G. Rosengarten, *William Reynolds, Rear Admiral U.S.N. John Fulton Reynolds, Major-General U.S.V. Colonel Fifth U.S. Infantry, A Memoir* (Philadelphia: J.B. Lippincott, 1880), 4–5; Nichols, *Toward Gettysburg*, 4; Riley, *For God's Sake*, 6–7.
17. Lydia Reynolds and Jane Reynolds, "Letters to a Brother, Annotated by Anne K. H. Cleaver," *Journal of the Lancaster Historical Society* 92, no. 1 (1989/90) [hereafter Cleaver, "Letters"]: 2; Nichols, *Toward Gettysburg*, 4; Riley, *For God's Sake*, 7.
18. Anne Hoffman Cleaver and E. Jeffrey Stann, eds., *Voyage to the Southern Ocean: The Letters of Lieutenant William Reynolds from the U.S. Exploring Expedition, 1838–1842* (Annapolis, MD: Naval Institute Press, 1998), 302–3; Reynolds Family Papers, Catharine (Kate), Correspondence February 15, 1833–May 16, 1847, letter September 25, 1846; Nichols, *Toward Gettysburg*, 29; Riley, *For God's Sake*, 13–14. Regarding John Reynolds's date of birth, many sources list September 20, 1820. However, Reynolds, in a letter written from Mexico on the occasion of the Battle of Monterrey, dated September 25, 1846, indicates, "The attack commenced on the 21st, my birthday, and lasted the greater part of the day."
19. Nichols, *Toward Gettysburg*, 4–5.
20. Franklin and Marshall College, Martin Library of Sciences, Archives & Special Collections, MS 24, Edward J. Nichols Collection, Typescript of John F. Reynolds Letters, Box 2–Folder 1 [hereafter Nichols Collection], John Reynolds [hereafter JFR] letter to his sister Lydia, December 19, 1933; Nichols, *Toward Gettysburg*, 3–6; Riley, *For God's Sake*, 7.
21. Nichols Collection, JFR letter to his sister Lydia, December 19, 1933, and letter to his father, dated January 18, 1834.

22. *Reynolds Memorial Addresses delivered before the Historical Society of Pennsylvania upon the occasion of the presentation of a portrait of Major General John F. Reynolds, March 8, 1880, Historical Society of Pennsylvania* (Philadelphia, PA: J.B. Lippincott & Company, 1880), Address of Mr. J.G. Rosengarten, 12 [hereafter *Rosengarten Address*]; Nichols, *Toward Gettysburg*, 7; Riley, *For God's Sake*, 7.
23. Nichols, *Toward Gettysburg*, 6.
24. Cleaver and Stann, *Voyage to the Southern Ocean*, xxviii; Cleaver, "Letters," 3.
25. Nichols, *Toward Gettysburg*, 4, 8–10; Riley, *For God's Sake*, 7.
26. Rosengarten, *William Reynolds*, 8; Nichols Collection, letter dated March 6, 1837, JFR to Secretary of War Lewis Cass; Nichols, *Toward Gettysburg*, 8–10; Riley, *For God's Sake*, 7–8.

3. Kate: Owego Orphan

27. Society of the Sacred Heart Archives, United States–Canada Province, St. Louis, Missouri, VII, D.3, Oversize Box 1, Eden Hall, School Register, Record of Students [hereafter: EH School Register]; Society of the Sacred Heart Archives, United States–Canada Province, St. Louis, Missouri, VII, D.3, Oversize Box 7, Eden Hall, Baptismal Register [hereafter EH Baptismal Register]; Province of the United States Admissions Book, RG 10-1, Daughters of Charity Archives, Province of St. Louise, Emmitsburg, Maryland [hereafter DoC Admissions Book]. Note: the proper abbreviation for the Daughters of Charity is D.C., DoC used here to avoid confusion with District of Columbia abbreviation. The genealogist who conducted the comprehensive family tree research for Kate Hewitt was Mary Stanford Pitkin [hereafter Pitkin research]. Eden Hall records list Kate's mother's first name as either "Jemina" or "Germina." Daughters of Charity records indicate "Jemima." Daughters of Charity admissions book lists Kate's mother's surname as "Maloney." Eden Hall Student Register lists her mother's surname as "Green." Eden Hall Baptismal Register listed mother's surname as "Green," but that was crossed out and "Maloney" was written in over top of "Green."
28. References to all census reports and city directories are from Pitkin research, much of which was derived from information available through Ancestry.com; 1850 U.S. Census, Warren County, Bradford Pennsylvania, p. 36; 1855, 1865, 1875, New York State Census, Owego County, NY; 1860 and 1870 U.S. Census, Tioga County, Owego NY; *Owego Gazette*, October 12, 1876, and December 26, 1878; *Albany (NY) Evening Journal*, August 7, 1877 (references to newspaper articles relate to items found on various online services to include, but not limited to: genealogybank.com,

newspaperarchive.com, newspapers.com, fultonhistory.com, chronicling america.loc.gov, nyshistoricnewspapers.org and newsbank.com). Federal and New York state census reports indicate Benjamin Hewitt spent his entire adult life in the Owego area except for one short foray to a not too distant community in northern Pennsylvania. The 1855 New York state census indicates Benjamin was born in Owego and lived in Owego for twenty-three years (the time he spent in Pennsylvania must have been brief). Benjamin died on December 18, 1878, at the age of forty-six. He is buried in South Owego Cemetery (see findagrave.com, Memorial ID 90226838).

29. Pitkin research.
30. Reynolds Family Papers, Eleanor Reynolds letter to her brother William, July 5, 1863.
31. DoC Admissions Book; Jeff Harding and Mary Stanford Pitkin, "Finding Kate," *Civil War Times* 59, no. 4 (August 2020): 56–63.
32. Tioga County, New York Historical Society [hereafter TCHS], email correspondence dated September 18, 2020, and correspondence with Peter C. Gordon, historian, Town of Owego, May 6, 2021. Per Gordon, the "village" of Owego was limited to 300 acres; the "town" consists of 106 square miles and includes many hamlets, the largest of which is Apalachin. Other hamlets include Campville, South Owego and Flemingville.
33. Charles Henry Veil, *The Memoirs of Charles Henry Veil*, Herman J. Viola, ed. (New York: Orion Books, 1993) 35; Reynolds Family Papers, Jane Gildersleeve Reynolds, letter to her brother William Reynolds, July 5, 1863; *Daily Alta* (San Francisco, CA), July 22, 1859 (any references to articles from the *Daily Alta, Shasta Courier, Sacramento Daily Union, Daily National Democrat* and *Stockton Independent* were derived from the California Digital Newspaper Collection, Center for Bibliographic Studies and Research, University of California, Riverside, http://cdnc.ucr.edu).
34. TCHS, email correspondence dated July 31 and September 29, 2020. The only Owego Academy rosters available are for the years ending in August 1852 and 1853 and one that covered the school's first two years of existence up to April 15, 1845. It is interesting to note, in considering Kate's extraordinary embroidery skills (to be detailed in a following chapter), that the "Winter Term" catalogue, dated January 2, 1852, listed "embroidery" as an optional course of instruction.

4. John: West Point

35. For a complete account of all four years of John Reynolds's life as a West Point cadet, see Kalina Ingham Hintz, "'My Military Life as a

Cadet Here…': The West Point Years of Maj. Gen. John F. Reynolds," *The Gettysburg Magazine*, July 2001, 23–38 [hereafter Hintz, "West Point Years"].

36. U.S. Military Academy, "A Brief History of West Point," https://www. westpoint.edu/about/history-of-west-point.

37. Hintz, "West Point Years," 27–28; Jeffrey Simpson, *Officers and Gentlemen* (Tarrytown, NY: Sleepy Hollow Press, 1982), 19, 21–23; William H. Baumer Jr., *West Point, Moulder of Men* (New York: D. Appleton-Century Company Inc., 1942), 14–15; Stephen E. Ambrose, *Duty, Honor, Country: A History of West Point* (Baltimore: Johns Hopkins Press, 1994), 24–37.

38. "Brief History of West Point"; Hintz, "West Point Years," 27; Ambrose, *Duty, Honor, Country*, 62–86; Thomas Fleming, "A New Country Starts a School for Soldiers," in Robert Cowley and Thomas Guinzburg, eds., *West Point: Two Centuries of Honor and Tradition* (New York: Warner Books, Inc., 2002), 30–44.

39. "Brief History of West Point"; Ambrose, *Duty, Honor, Country*, 62–86; Fleming, "New Country Starts a School," 30–44; James L. Morrison Jr., "Educating the Civil War Generals: West Point, 1833–1861," *Military Affairs* 38, no. 3 (October 1974), 108–11. Major Richard Delafield served as superintendent from 1838 to 1845. See Mark M. Boatner III, *The Civil War Dictionary*, rev. ed. (New York: Random House, 1991), entry for Delafield, Richard, 232 [hereafter Boatner, *Civil War Dictionary*]. It is interesting to note that Delafield also served as superintendent from 1856 until March 1, 1861. This means that the man who was superintendent while Reynolds was a cadet was also the superintendent when Reynolds returned to West Point as commandant in September 1860.

40. Reynolds Family Papers and Nichols Collection, JFR letter to his brother William Reynolds, August 20, 1837; Nichols, *Toward Gettysburg*, 10; Hintz, "West Point Years," 31.

41. Reynolds Family Papers, JFR letter to his sister Lydia Reynolds, April 10, 1839; Hintz, "West Point Years," 30; Riley, *For God's Sake*, 8.

42. Reynolds Family Papers, JFR letter to his sister Lydia Reynolds, January 1, 1841, JFR letter to his sister Jane, March 8, 1841; Nichols, *Toward Gettysburg*, 12–13; Riley, *For God's Sake*, 8; Hintz, "West Point Years," 32, 37.

43. Nichols, *Toward Gettysburg*, 11, 13; Riley, *For God's Sake*, 8; Loski, "For the Country's Sake," 39. During Reynolds's time at West Point, he would also have encountered lower and upper classmen who went on to play key roles in the Civil War, including the likes of George Thomas, Richard Ewell, James Longstreet, Ulysses S. Grant and Winfield Scott Hancock.

44. George W. Cullum, *Biographical Register of the Officers and Graduates of the U. S. Military Academy*, 3 vols. (Boston and New York, 1891), vol. 2, 92–

93; Nichols, *Toward Gettysburg*, 11; Riley, *For God's Sake*, 8; Hintz, "West Point Years," 35; John C. Waugh, *The Class of 1846, From West Point to Appomattox: Stonewall Jackson, George McClellan and Their Brothers* (New York: Ballentine Books, 1966), 126; Ambrose, *Duty, Honor, Country*, 165; Joseph Pearson Farley, *West Point in the Early Sixties* (Troy, NY: Pafraets Book Company, 1902), 69; Thomas Rowland, ed., "Letters of a Virginia Cadet at West Point, 1859–1861," *South Atlantic Quarterly* 15 (January–October 1916), 206.

45. Hintz, "West Point Years," 34, 36, 39; Reynolds Family Papers, JFR letter to his sister Lydia Reynolds, May 24, 1840; Riley, *For God's Sake*, 8; James L. Morrison Jr., *"The Best School": West Point, 1833–1866* (Kent, OH: Kent State University Press), 160–63.

46. *Rosengarten Address*, 12; Cullum, *Biographical Register*, 92; Nichols, *Toward Gettysburg*, 13; Riley, *For God's Sake*, 9; Hintz, "West Point Years," 38.

47. *2000 Register of Graduates and Former Cadets of the United States Military Academy West Point New York* (Class of 1900 Centennial Edition) (West Point, NY: Association of Graduates West Point, 1999), list of class mottoes, 5–37; Hintz, "West Point Years," 38.

5. John: Army Life and the Mexican War

48. Reynolds Family Papers and Nichols Collection, JFR letter to his father, October 3, 1841; Nichols, *Toward Gettysburg*, 14; Riley, *For God's Sake*, 9. The ranking officers either had not yet reported or were in Baltimore at the moment he wrote.

49. Nichols, *Toward Gettysburg*, 14–68; Riley, *For God's Sake*, 9–21; Loski, "For the Country's Sake," 39–40.

50. Nichols, *Toward Gettysburg*, 15; Riley, *For God's Sake*, 9–10.

51. Nichols, *Toward Gettysburg*, 18; Riley, *For God's Sake*, 10.

52. Nichols, *Toward Gettysburg*, 17; Riley, *For God's Sake*, 10.

53. Nichols, *Toward Gettysburg*, 22; Riley, *For God's Sake*, 11; Texas State Historical Association [hereafter TSHA], "Fort Brown," https://www.tshaonline.org/handbook/entries/fort-brown-2; National Park Service [hereafter NPS], "Fort Brown," https://www.nps.gov/places/fort-brown.htm; NPS, "Fort Texas/Fort Brown," https://www.nps.gov/paal/learn/historyculture/siegeofforttexas.htm. "Seeing the Elephant" was a frequently used euphemism for seeing battle. Today, "Point Isabel" is Port Isabel.

54. Nichols, *Toward Gettysburg*, 23; Riley, *For God's Sake*, 11; TSHA, "Fort Brown"; NPS, "Fort Brown"; NPS, "Fort Texas/Fort Brown."

55. Nichols, *Toward Gettysburg*, 23–24; Riley, *For God's Sake*, 11; TSHA, "Fort Brown"; NPS, "Fort Brown"; NPS, "Fort Texas/Fort Brown."

56. Nichols, *Toward Gettysburg*, 23–24, Riley, *For God's Sake*, 11; TSHA, "Fort Brown"; NPS, "Fort Brown"; NPS, "Fort Texas/Fort Brown."

57. Nichols, *Toward Gettysburg*, 23–24; Riley, *For God's Sake*, 11; TSHA, "Fort Brown"; NPS, "Fort Brown"; NPS, "Fort Texas/Fort Brown." Fort Brown ultimately lent its name to the town established where it once stood, Brownsville, Texas.

58. Reynolds Family Papers and Nichols Collection, JFR letter to his sister Jane, June 12, 1846; Nichols, *Toward Gettysburg*, 25; Riley, *For God's Sake*, 11–12; NPS, "Fort Brown"; NPS, "Fort Texas/Fort Brown." Per Riley, Reynolds's promotion involved a transfer to Company G, then stationed in Florida, but Reynolds arranged to stay on "detached service" with Company E. Obviously, he did not want to miss the war and his chance at glory.

59. Reynolds Family Papers, JFR letter to his sister Catharine (Kate), September 25, 1846; Nichols, *Toward Gettysburg*, 29; Riley, *For God's Sake*, 14–15; Stephen A. Carney, *Gateway South: The Campaign for Monterrey* (Washington, D.C.: U.S. Army Center of Military History, 2005), 22–23.

60. Reynolds Family Papers, JFR letter to his sister Catharine (Kate), September 25, 1846; *Rosengarten Address*, 13–14 (quotes from JFR letter of December 6, 1846, that per Nichols, was lost, see Nichols, *Toward Gettysburg*, 229, note 47); Nichols, *Toward Gettysburg*, 30, 32–33; Riley, *For God's Sake*, 14–15; Carney, *Gateway South*, 24–26.

61. Nichols, *Toward Gettysburg*, 33.

62. Nichols, *Toward Gettysburg*, 35–36; Riley, *For God's Sake*, 15–16; Stephen A. Carney, *Desperate Stand: The Battle of Buena Vista* (Washington, D.C.: U.S. Army Center of Military History, 2015), 2–19. Reynolds was serving under Thomas W. Sherman, as his former battery commander, Braxton Bragg, due to casualties in prior actions, had been transferred to another battery that famously served quite heroically during the climax of the battle. Each of the officers serving in Sherman's Battery at Buena Vista, including John Reynolds, attained rank during the Civil War. In the Union army, there were Reynolds and George Thomas (the Rock of Chickamauga), and in the Confederate army there were Samuel French and Robert S. Garnett (first Confederate general officer killed in battle).

63. Reynolds Family Papers and Nichols Collection, JFR letter to his sister Jane, March 1, 1847; Nichols, *Toward Gettysburg*, 39; Riley, *For God's Sake*, 15–16.

64. Reynolds Family Papers and Nichols Collection, JFR letter to his sister Jane, March 1, 1847; Nichols, *Toward Gettysburg*, 39–40; Riley, *For God's Sake*, 15–16; David Lavender, *Climax at Buena Vista: The Decisive Battle of the Mexican-American War* (Philadelphia: University of Pennsylvania Press, 2003), 186; John S.D. Eisenhower, *So Far from God: The U.S. War with Mexico*

1846–1848 (New York: Random House, Inc., 1989), 187; K. Jack Bauer, *The Mexican War, 1846–1848* (Lincoln: University of Nebraska Press, 1992), 210–12.

65. James Henry Carlton, *The Battle of Buena Vista: With the Operations of the "Army of Occupation" for One Month* (New York, New York: Harper and Brothers, 1848), 92–93, 101 (hereafter Carlton *Buena Vista*); Samuel Gibbs French, *Two Wars: An Autobiography of General Samuel G. French* (Nashville, Tennessee: Confederate Veteran, 1901), 80; Nichols, *Toward Gettysburg*, 40–41; Riley, *For God's Sake*, 15–16; Carney, *Desperate Stand*, 30; Lavender, *Climax at Buena Vista*, 187–208; Eisenhower, *So Far from God*, 185–187; Bauer, *Mexican War*, 216–17.

66. Carlton, *Buena Vista*, 109–19; Nichols, *Toward Gettysburg*, 42–43; Riley, *For God's Sake*, 15–16; Robert Benjamin Smith, "Battle of Buena Vista," https://www.historynet.com/battle-of-buena-vista.htm; Carney, *Desperate Stand*, 31–35; Robert Selph Henry, *The Story of the Mexican War* (New York: Bobbs-Merrill Company Inc., 1950), 252–53; Bauer, *Mexican War*, 216–17; Lavender, *Climax at Buena Vista*, 208–11; Eisenhower, *So Far from God*, 187–90.

67. Reynolds Family Papers and Nichols Collection, letter to his sister Jane, March 1, 1847; Nichols, *Toward Gettysburg*, 42–43; Riley, *For God's Sake*, 15–16.

6. Kate: California Girl

68. Museum of the City of San Francisco, sfmuseum.org; Katherine H. Chandler, "San Francisco at Statehood," *San Francisco Chronicle*, September 9, 1900.

69. Museum of the City of San Francisco, sfmuseum.org; Katherine H. Chandler, "San Francisco at Statehood," *San Francisco Chronicle*, September 9, 1900.

70. San Francisco Memories, sanfranciscomemories.com. The What Cheer House operated from 1866 to 1891.

71. Mary R. Maloney, "Dear Kate," *Journal of the Lancaster County Historical Society* 65, no. 3 (Summer 1961): 136–43 (Maloney subsequently published numerous variations of this article in various newspapers and journals, including *American Heritage*); Pitkin research, there are no records in either city directories or census reports that list a "G.R. Woodward" in the San Francisco area in the 1850s or 1860s.

72. Pitkin research; marriage announcement, *San Francisco (CA) Bulletin*, April 13, 1860; *Providence (RI) Daily Journal*, May 15, 1862; 1850 U.S. Census for Bradford County, Pennsylvania.

73. Pitkin research; New York State Census for Tioga County, 1855.

74. *Daily Alta*, October 2, 1857; Pitkin research; James Newell Arnold, *Rhode Island Vital Extracts*, 1636–1850. 21 volumes (Providence, RI: Narragansett Historical Publishing Company, 1891–1912), digitized images from New England Historic Genealogical Society, Boston, Massachusetts; *Manufacturers and Farmers Journal* (Providence, RI), September 7, 1857; *Providence (RI) Daily Journal*, September 7, 1857; Frank Burns, *The Two Catherines: An Extraordinary True Story from the American Civil War* (Dublin: Original Writing, 2015), 12. Woodward's oldest daughter, Sarah, was only nine years old, and their youngest child, daughter Mary, was born in 1857. The SS *Star of the West* is the same ship that would end up being fired on in an effort to resupply Fort Sumter on January 9, 1861.

7. *John: Go West Young Man*

75. William Frederic Worner, "Dinner Declined by Major John Fulton Reynolds," *Journal of the Lancaster County Historical Society* 34, no. 9 (1930): 213–15; Ezra J. Warner, *Generals in Blue: Lives of the Union Commanders* (Baton Rouge: Louisiana State Press, 1999), 396; Nichols, *Toward Gettysburg*, 52; Riley, *For God's Sake*, 16–17. Reynolds was awarded two brevet promotions for his gallantry and bravery in the Mexican War, one to captain for his actions at Monterrey and another to major for his actions at Buena Vista.
76. Reynolds Family Papers, JFR letter to his sister Harriot, January 31, 1849; Nichols, *Toward Gettysburg*, 53–54; Riley, *For God's Sake*, 18.
77. Reynolds Family Papers, JFR letter to his sister Jane, January 1, 1848; Nichols, *Toward Gettysburg*, 50–51; Riley, *For God's Sake*, 16.
78. Reynolds Family Papers, JFR letter to his sister Harriot, January 31, 1849; Nichols, *Toward Gettysburg*, 55; Riley, *For God's Sake*, 17–18.
79. Nichols, *Toward Gettysburg*, 56; Riley, *For God's Sake*, 18.
80. Reynolds Family Papers, JFR letter to his sister Eleanor, November 1, 1853; Nichols, *Toward Gettysburg*, 55–56.
81. Nichols, *Toward Gettysburg*, 56; Riley, *For God's Sake*, 18.
82. John Stewart, *The Wreck of the San Francisco* (Jefferson, NC: McFarland & Company Inc., 2018), 1, 8, 26, 62–96, 108, 229–37; author email correspondence with meteorologist Dr. Jon Nese, dated June 10, 2021; HURDAT, National Hurricane Center; "Total Loss of the San Francisco," *New York Daily Times*, January 14, 1854; "Total Loss of the Steamship San Francisco," *New York Herald*, January 14, 1854. It is interesting to note that the ship's master, Commodore James T. Watkins, who survived the sinking of the SS *San Francisco*, was also in command of the vessel that brought John Reynolds and Kate Hewitt from San Francisco to Panama in the summer of 1860.

83. Reynolds Family Papers, JFR to sister Eleanor, March 28, 1854; Stewart, *Wreck of the San Francisco*, 213; Nichols, *Toward Gettysburg*, 56–57; Riley, *For God's Sake*, 18.

84. Reynolds Family Papers, JFR to either sister Eleanor or Hal, March 28, 1855; Nichols, *Toward Gettysburg*, 57–59; Riley, *For God's Sake*, 18.

85. Reynolds Family Papers, JFR letter to his sisters, August 27, 1855; Nichols, *Toward Gettysburg*, 59–60.

86. Reynolds Family Papers, JFR letters to Eleanor, November 1, 1855, and December 18, 1855; Nichols, *Toward Gettysburg*, 60; Riley, *For God's Sake*, 19; Kelsey Wallace, "The Dangerous Life of a Columbia River Bar Pilot," OPB News, https://www.opb.org/artsandlife/article/columbia-river-bar-pilots-oregon-field-guide/.

87. Reynolds Family Papers, JFR letter to his sister Eleanor, December, 18, 1855; Erasmus D. Keyes, *Fifty Years' Observation of Men and Events, Civil and Military* (New York: Charles Scriber's Sons, 1884), 250–51; Nichols, *Toward Gettysburg*, 60; Riley, *For God's Sake*, 19.

88. Reynolds Family Papers, JFR letter to his sister Eleanor, December 18, 1855; Keyes, *Fifty Years' Observation*, 250–51; Nichols, *Toward Gettysburg*, 60.

89. Reynolds Family Papers, JFR letter to his sister Eleanor, January 11, 1856; City of Port Orford, "About Port Orford," https://portorford.org/about-port-orford/.

90. Reynolds Family Papers, JFR to his sisters, June 19, 1956, and presentation letter, "Citizens of Port Orford," Oregon Territory, to JFR, July 31, 1856; Nichols, *Toward Gettysburg*, 61; Riley, *For God's Sake*, 19–20. Numerous Reynolds family descendants contacted by this author are unaware of the whereabouts of this watch.

91. Nichols, *Toward Gettysburg*, 62–68; Riley, *For God's Sake*, 20–21; Loski, "For the Country's Sake," 40.

92. *Daily Alta*, Pacific Mail Steamship Company advertisement, July 20, 1860; "Passengers by the Golden Age," *Daily Bee* (Sacramento, CA), July 23, 1860; Nichols, *Toward Gettysburg*, 70; Riley, *For God's Sake*, 21.

8. Kate: Revelation and Scandal

93. "Passengers by the Golden Age"; "Letter from New York," *Daily Bee*, September 15, 1860.

94. "Passengers by the Golden Age"; "Letter from New York," *Daily Bee*, September 15, 1860; *Sacramento Daily Union*, July 21, 1859; *Shasta Courier*, July 30, 1859.

95. Cindy L. Baker, MA, "Sacramento's Sophisticated Ladies: Prostitution in 1860" *Golden Notes* 41, no. 2 (Summer 1995): 9–38; Pitkin research, U.S.

Census for Sacramento, California, 1860, 101 (dated June 21); *Taylor's Sacramento Directory, for the Year Commencing October 1858*, compiled by L.S. Taylor (Sacramento, CA: L.S. Taylor, 1858), 31; *Sacramento City Directory, for the Year A.D. 1860*, compiled by D.S. Cutler (Sacramento, CA: D.S. Cutter and Co., 1859), 47, 104; *The Sacramento City Directory for the Years 1861 and 1862*, compiled by H.J. Bidleman (Sacramento, CA: John J. Murphy, 1861), 13, 126, 137; email correspondence from James C. Scott, librarian/archivist, Special Collections, Sacramento Public Library, dated May 8 and 20, 2021.

96. Melissa Hope Ditmore, *Encyclopedia of Prostitution and Sex Work*, vol. 1. (Westport, CT: Greenwood Press, 2006), 21; Alexy Simmons, "Red Light Ladies in the American West: Entrepreneurs and Companions," *Australian Journal of Historical Archaeology* 7 (1989): 63–69.

97. "Letter From New York," *Daily Bee*, September 15, 1860. Recent scholarship disputes the origin of the Twain quote.

98. *Daily National Democrat* (Marysville, CA), July 22, 1859, and August 18, 1859; *Sacramento Daily Union*, July 21, 1859.

99. Pitkin research, U.S. Census for El Dorado County, California, 1850; *Shasta Courier*, July 30, 1859; "California Legislative Report," *Daily Alta*, October 6, 1855; *Daily Bee*, February 22, 1860.

100. *Daily National Democrat* (Marysville, CA), July 22, 1859; *Sacramento Daily Union*, July 2, 1859.

101. *Daily Alta*, July 22, 1859; *Danville (VT) North Star*, September 3, 1859.

102. *Daily Alta*, July 22, 1859; *San Francisco Bulletin*, July 22, 1859.

103. *Daily Alta*, July 22, 1859; *Arkansas True Democrat* (Little Rock, AR), September 7, 1859.

104. *Daily Alta*, July 22, 1859; *Arkansas True Democrat* (Little Rock, AR), September 7, 1859.

9. John and Kate: A Fateful Encounter

105. "Letter from New York"; *Daily Alta*, July 18, 21 and 22, 1860.

106. "Passengers by the Golden Age"; "Letter From New York"; "Passenger List SS *North Star*," *Daily Bee*, August 13, 1860; Harding and Pitkin, "Finding Kate," 56–63.

107. Pitkin research, U.S. Census for Sacramento, California, 1860, 101; EH School Register; Annual Letters, Society of the Sacred Heart, 1859–1862, Eden Hall, 343–46 [hereafter EH Annual Letters].

108. "Letter from New York."

109. Ibid.

110. Ibid.

111. *New York Tribune*, passenger list transcription for SS *North Star*, August 13, 1860; New York Passenger and Crew Lists 1820–1957, ancestry.com.

112. Reynolds Family Papers, Jane Reynolds Gildersleeve, letter to her brother William Reynolds, July 5, 1863; "Later From Oregon," *Daily Alta*, July 18, 1860.

10. John and Kate: Engagement and a Last Promise

113. Returns from U.S. Military Posts 1800–1916, Records of the United States Army Continental Commands, 1821–1920 (National Archives Microfilm Publication, Record Group 393, M 617, Roll 1414, U.S. Military Academy, Jan. 1853–Dec. 1865), Officers, Professors, &c., of the Military Academy, and Commissioned Officers of the Post present and absent, accounted for by name, West Point, New York, September, 1860 (viewed on Fold3), (hereafter WP Post Return, September, 1860, RG 393, M 617, Roll 1414); "Officers Ordered to West Point," *New York Herald*, August 31, 1860; Reynolds Family Papers, JFR letter to his sister Eleanor Reynolds, September 20, 1860.

114. Reynold family descendants generously provided the author with a detailed description of John Reynolds's West Point ring. There were no standard class rings in 1841, and each cadet selected his own individual design. See West Point Bicentennial, "Class Rings, Miniatures, and A-Pins," https://www.west-point.org/family/bicent/rings.html.

115. Reynolds Family Papers, Jane Reynolds Gildersleeve letter to her brother William Reynolds, July 5, 1863.

116. Ibid.; Eleanor Reynolds to her brother William, July 5, 1863.

117. Reynolds Family Papers, JFR letter to his sisters, December 10, 1860.

118. Reynolds Family Papers, Jane Reynolds Gildersleeve letter to her brother William Reynolds, July 5, 1863; Eleanor Reynolds to her brother William, July 5, 1863.

119. Reynolds Family Papers, Jane Reynolds Gildersleeve letter to her brother William Reynolds, July 5, 1863; Eleanor Reynolds to her brother William, July 5, 1863; William Riddle, letter to Lt. Bouvier, August 4, 1863.

120. Reynolds Family Papers, Jane Reynolds Gildersleeve letter to her brother William Reynolds, July 5, 1863; Eleanor Reynolds to her brother William, July 5, 1863; William Riddle, letter to Lt. Bouvier, August 4, 1863.

11. John: Return to the Point

121. WP Post Return, September, 1860, RG 393, M 617, Roll 1414; "Officers Ordered to West Point," *New York Herald*, August 31, 1860; Reynolds Family Papers, JFR to his sister Eleanor, September 20, 1860; Nichols, *Toward Gettysburg*, 70–71.
122. Reynolds Family Papers, JFR to his brother Samuel, November 19, 1860.
123. Reynolds Family Papers, JFR letter to his sister Eleanor, April 25, 1861; James S. Robbins, *Last in Their Class: Custer, Pickett and the Goats of West Point* (New York: Encounter Books, 2006), 199.
124. Reynolds Family Papers, JFR letter to his brother Sam, November 19, 1860; Riley, *For God's Sake*, 21–22; Robbins, *Last in Their Class*, 204. Due to the Civil War, West Point graduated two classes in 1861, one on May 6 and the second on June 30.

12. Kate: Salvation and Redemption

125. EH School Register; EH Baptismal Register. No documentation exists to indicate where Kate and Catherine Dunn (possibly aka Mary North) were between August 13, 1860, and November 10, 1860.
126. EH Annual Letters.
127. Society of the Sacred Heart Archives, United States–Canada Province, St. Louis, Missouri ,VII, D.2, Oversize Box 7, Eden Hall, Pupils Ledger (Legal and Financial), 1855–1886 [hereafter EH Pupils Ledger]; CPI Inflation Calculator, https://www.bls.gov/data/inflation_calculator.htm; U.S. Bureau of Labor Statistics, officialdata.org.
128. The notes in Catherine Dunn's Eden Hall records list her as being "married" sometime after leaving the school. It seems probable that she married sometime prior to 1870, because she was not living in Albany with Kate Hewitt at the time of the 1870 U.S. Census.
129. Reynolds Family Papers, Eleanor letter to her brother William Reynolds, July 5; Jane Reynolds Gildersleeve, letter to her brother William Reynolds, July 5, 1863; Pitkin research; 1850 U.S. Census and 1855 New York State Census.

13. John: Civil War—Through the Ranks

130. Reynolds Family Papers, JFR to his sister Eleanor, July 1, 1861, and July 15, 1861; Nichols, *Toward Gettysburg*, 75–76, 21–23; Warner, *Generals in Blue*, 396; Riley, *For God's Sake*, 22–23. Reynolds's promotion was backdated to August 20, 1861. This appointment was a volunteer army commission

and not a regular army promotion; John Reynolds remained a lieutenant colonel in the regular army at this time.

131. Reynolds Family Papers, JFR letter to his sisters, September 17, 1861; Riley, *For God's Sake*, 22–23; Nichols, *Toward Gettysburg*, 75–76, 235n38; U.S. War Department, *The War of the Rebellion: A Compilation of the Official Records of the Union and Confederate Armies* [hereafter *OR*], 128 parts in 70 volumes and atlas (Washington, D.C.: Government Printing Office, 1880–1901), series 1, vol. 4, 581, 612, and vol. 51, part I, section 1, 469–80.

132. Reynolds Family Papers, JFR letter to Eleanor Reynolds, January 12, 1862, and January 17, 1862; Nichols, *Toward Gettysburg*, 82–83.

133. Stephen W. Sears, *To the Gates of Richmond* (New York: Ticknor & Fields, 1992), 203; Boatner, *Civil War*, 476; History.com editors, "Peninsula Campaign," https://www.history.com/topics/american-civil-war/peninsula-campaign; Reynolds Family Papers, JFR letter to his sister Eleanor, June 10, 1862; Nichols, *Toward Gettysburg*, 87; Riley, *For God's Sake*, 25. Lee assumed command on June 1, 1862. From that point on, this army became known as the Army of Northern Virginia.

134. Nichols, *Toward Gettysburg*, 90; Clifford Dowdey, *The Seven Days: The Emergence of Lee* (Canada: Little, Brown & Company Limited, 1864), 182–91; Riley, *For God's Sake*, 26; Sears, *To the Gates*, 202.

135. Nichols, *Toward Gettysburg*, 91–92; Dowdey, *Seven Days*, 182–91; Riley, *For God's Sake*, 26–28; Sears, *To the Gates*, 203–9; Library of Congress, "Battle of Beaver Dam Creek, Mechanicsville, Hanover County, VA," https://www.loc.gov/item/va2109/. The number of Confederates engaged at Mechanicsville is estimated at 11,000 men, an estimated 1300–1,475 causalities. The total number of Federals engaged is estimated at 14,000 men, who suffered an estimated 361–400 casualties; these numbers include not only the Pennsylvania Reserves (estimated at 9,500 men/200 casualties) but other Union forces engaged during the battle as well.

136. Robert K. Krick, *Civil War Weather in Virginia* (Tuscaloosa: University of Alabama Press, 2007), 60–61; Reynolds Family Papers, JFR letter to his sister Eleanor, July 3, 1862; Nichols, *Toward Gettysburg*, 94–97; Riley, *For God's Sake*, 28–29; Sears, *To the Gates*, 252. Sears relies on an account indicating Reynolds was captured after having fallen asleep on the night of the 27–28, awaiting his chance to escape when the sun rose. Sears indicates Reynolds was still sleeping when captured on the morning of June 28, but this differs from Reynolds's own account, which indicates he was in the midst of trying to "regain the position of our lines" when captured. Certainly exhaustion might have played a role here, but from what this author has read of John Reynolds's character and commitment

to duty, nothing suggests the possibility he would have voluntarily decided to sleep through the morning in the midst of such a situation.

137. Edward J. Nichols, "The Military Record of General John F. Reynolds," *Journal of the Lancaster County Historical Society* 63, no. 3 (1959): 6; Nichols, *Toward Gettysburg*, 97–99; Riley, *For God's Sake*, 29–30; Warner, *Generals in Blue*, 397. Per Nichols, in *Toward Gettysburg*, 238n56, General Order No. 118 indicates Reynolds was exchanged for Brigadier General Lloyd Tilghman. The Reynolds family members believed Reynolds was exchanged for Brigadier General William Barksdale, who was also destined to die at Gettysburg, but evidence indicates it was Tilghman. Reynolds was exchanged on August 8, 1862.

138. Nichols, "Military Record," 6; Nichols, *Toward Gettysburg*, 101–2; Warner, *Generals in Blue*, 289–90 and 397; Riley, *For God's Sake*, 30. Reynolds replaced McCall, who was captured on June 30 during the Battle of Glendale (Frayser's Farm). McCall was exchanged on August 18 but was not well upon his return and was sent to Washington, D.C.

139. Nichols, "Military Record," 7; Nichols, *Toward Gettysburg*, 103–15; Riley, *For God's Sake*, 30–32; John J. Hennessy, *Return to Bull Run: The Campaign and Battle of Second Manassas* (New York: Simon and Schuster, 1993), 81; *OR*, ser. 1, vol. 12, part 2, 392, 397.

140. Jackson made a name for himself on the reverse slope (southeast) of the hill, while Reynolds's troops fought on the forward slope (northwest) of the hill.

141. Hennessy, *Return to Bull Run*, 407–10; Krick, *Civil War Weather*, 66–67.

142. Letter, J. H. Masten to the *Warren Mail*, September 20, 1862; Evan Morrison Wodward [from old catalog], *Our Campaigns* (Philadelphia: J.E. Potter, 1865), 186–87; OR, ser. 1, vol. 12, part 2, 192, 587–88, 590; Nichols, *Toward Gettysburg*, 115–16; Riley, *For God's Sake*, 32; Hennessy, *Return to Bull Run*, 412–13; Howard Thomson and William H. Rauch, *History of the "Bucktails" Kane Rifle Regiment of the Pennsylvania Reserve Corps* (Philadelphia: Electric Printing Co., 1906), 192.

143. Hennessy, *Return to Bull Run*, 414–24; *OR*, ser. 1, vol. 12, part 2, 341–42, 532; Nichols, "Military Record," 7. Sykes's men were regular army, not volunteers, hence the reason for the description "disciplined."

14. John: Civil War—Corps Command

144. Nichols, *Toward Gettysburg*, 123–40 and 147; Riley, *For God's Sake*, 33–34; NPS, "Order of Battle Fredericksburg Reserve Grand Division," https:// www.nps.gov/frsp/learn/historyculture/order-of-battle-fredericksburg-reserve-grand-division.htm. Reynolds retained command when Major

General Hooker returned to the army, as Hooker was placed in command of the "Center Grand Division" (a "Grand Division" contained two corps). Prior to Fredericksburg, the Army of the Potomac was reorganized into three Grand Divisions. Reynolds's First Corps and William F. Smith's Sixth Corps formed the Left Grand Division under the command of Major General William B. Franklin, and Major General Edwin "Bull" Sumner commanded the Right Grand Division. Hooker commanded the Center Grand Division.

145. Nichols, *Toward Gettysburg*, 150–53; Riley, *For God's Sake*, 35–37; NPS, "Battle of Fredericksburg History: The River Crossing," https://www.nps.gov/frsp/learn/historyculture/fburg-hist-crossing.htm; Krick, *Civil War Weather*, 78.

146. NPS, "Battle of Fredericksburg History: Prospect Hill," https://www.nps.gov/frsp/learn/historyculture/hist-fburg-prospect.htm; Reynolds Family Papers, JFR to his sisters, December 17, 1862; Haskell, *Battle of Gettysburg*, 14; Nichols, *Toward Gettysburg*, 150–54; Riley, *For God's Sake*, 38–39.

147. Reynolds Family Papers, JFR letter to his sisters, January 23, 1863; Nichols, *Toward Gettysburg*, 157. It is important to note that news of John's death could not have reached Kate prior to July 2, yet she showed up at John's sister's home in Philadelphia on July 3 to view John's remains. This seems to lend credence to the fact that she was living somewhere in Philadelphia at the time, perhaps near Eden Hall.

148. Nichols, *Toward Gettysburg*, 161; Reynolds Family Papers, JFR letter to his sister Eleanor Reynolds, February 24, 1863.

149. Coddington, *Gettysburg Campaign*, 31–34; Riley, *For God's Sake*, 40–41; Nichols, *Toward Gettysburg*, 158–79.

150. Reynolds Family Papers, Eleanor Reynolds letter to her nephew Colonel J.F. Landis, August 20, 1913; Colonel Charles S. Wainwright, *A Diary of Battle: The Personal Journals of Colonel Charles S. Wainwright, 1861–1865*, ed. Allan Nevins (New York: Harcourt, Brace & World, 1962), 229; Nichols, *Toward Gettysburg*, 220–23; Riley, *For God's Sake*, 42–44; Coddington, *Gettysburg Campaign*, 37, 611–12.

151. Nichols, *Toward Gettysburg*, 184–85; Riley, *For God's Sake*, 44; Wayne E. Motts and Michael A. Riley, *Reynolds* (Gettysburg, PA: Dale Gallon Historical Art, Inc., 1997); Coddington, *Gettysburg Campaign*, 70 and 122; *OR*, ser. 1, vol. 27, part 3, 69–73, 305, 307. Coddington, per the *OR*, as cited here, indicates Howard and the cavalry (under General Pleasonton) were part of Reynolds's right wing command.

152. Reynolds Family Papers, Mary Catherine Reynolds to Harriot S. Reynolds, July 1, 1863; Nichols, *Toward Gettysburg*, 182–84, 220–21.

153. Nichols, *Toward Gettysburg*, 190–91; Riley, *For God's Sake*, 45; Coddington, *Gettysburg Campaign*, 209.
154. Hartwig, "At Great Risk," 13.

15. Kate: Farewell John

155. Reynolds Family Papers, Eleanor Reynolds letter to her brother William Reynolds, July 5, 1863; *Philadelphia Inquirer*, second edition, July 2, 1863.
156. EH Annual Letters.
157. Reynolds Family Papers, Eleanor Reynolds, letter to her brother William Reynolds, July 5, 1863.
158. Reynolds Family Papers, Jane Reynolds Gildersleeve, letter to her brother William Reynolds, July 5, 1863.
159. Reynolds Family Papers, Eleanor Reynolds, letter to her brother William Reynolds, July 5, 1863.
160. Reynolds Family Papers, Jane Reynolds Gildersleeve, letter to her brother William Reynolds, July 5, 1863; William Riddle letter to Lt. Bouvier, August 4, 1863.
161. Reynolds Family Papers, Jane Reynolds Gildersleeve, letter to her brother William Reynolds, July 5, 1863. The reader will recall that "Hal" was John's second-youngest sister, Harriot. Also, "Friday" was July 3, 1863.
162. Reynolds Family Papers, Jane Reynolds Gildersleeve, letter to her brother William Reynolds, July 5, 1863; Eleanor Reynolds letter to her brother William Reynolds, July 5, 1863; and William Riddle to Lt. Bouvier, August 4, 1863. Over the years, historians have either confused or embellished the description of the "Dear Kate" ring (some even speculating the ring was an Irish claddagh ring—though no primary source supports this claim) and other items found on General Reynolds's remains. Reynolds staff member and aide-de-camp Major William Riddle's firsthand account is the best and most reliable source of information pertaining to the ring, heart and cross. On August 4, 1863, just one month after the battle, he indicated, "On the General's little finger was that gold ring I spoke of bearing inside the words 'Dear Kate,' which he valued very highly. I remember hearing Col. Kingsbury speak of the great anxiety he exhibited when the ring was once lost for a time. He wore about his neck by a short silken string those two emblems of the Catholic Faith—heart & cross—which I remember seeing once during his life time."
163. Reynolds Family Papers, Jane Reynolds Gildersleeve, letter to her brother William Reynolds, July 5, 1863.
164. Ibid.

165. Ibid. John Reynolds's sister Eleanor indicated that she kept the small gold ring also known as the "Dear Kate" ring. Numerous Reynolds family descendants contacted by this author are unaware of the whereabouts of this ring.

16. Kate: The Daughters of Charity—Emmitsburg

166. DoC, daughtersofcharity.org.
167. Seton Shrine, SetonShrine.org; Wikipedia, "Elizabeth Ann Seton," https://en.wikipedia.org/wiki/Elizabeth_Ann_Seton; DoC, daughtersofcharity.org.
168. Seton Shrine, SetonShrine.org; Wikipedia, "Elizabeth Ann Seton," https://en.wikipedia.org/wiki/Elizabeth_Ann_Seton; DoC, daughtersofcharity.org. She was canonized on Sunday, September 14, 1975, in St. Peter's Square by Pope Paul VI.
169. emmitsburg.net.
170. DoC Admissions Book; Nichols Collection; Franklin and Marshall College Archives and Special Collections, Abstract of letter from Sister Josephine, Secretary, Sisters of Charity, St. Joseph's House, Emmitsburg, Maryland, dated April 12, 1957, to Dr. John V. Miller (from copy forwarded to Edward J. Nichols).
171. DoC Admissions Book. There is a possibility that Huntington, New York, had somehow been confused (in the original document) with Huntingdon Valley, Pennsylvania, which was much closer to Philadelphia and therefore seems more logical.
172. DoC Admissions Book; email correspondence with Daughters of Charity provincial archivist, dated June 9, 2020, and December, 29, 2020; Daughters of Charity Dictionary, https://daughters-of-charity.com/dictionary/. Kate Hewitt's period of service at Mount Hope was estimated by the current Daughters of Charity archivist to have been at least three months, likely December 1863 to Februay 1864 and perhaps beginning as many as three months earlier.
173. The DoC Admissions Book lists a few different dates, in various parts of the document, but email correspondence from the current DoC archivist, dated August 3, 2020, confirms March 17 as Kate's date of entry.
174. Veil, *Memoirs*, 34–36; Kalina Anderson, "The Girl He Left Behind," *America's Civil War*, July 1999; Reynolds Family Papers, Eleanor Reynolds letter to Charles McClure, February 16, 1864; GNMP Veil–McConaughy letter (recall this letter was written on April 7, 1864); John Reynolds Participant Account File, Gettysburg National Military Park letter, Charles H. Veil to W. D. Holzworth, January 8, 1882. In Veil's letter to McConaughy, Veil implies that he had recently visited Gettysburg to mark

the spot where General Reynolds fell. This was the visit he made with Reynolds's sisters and was the same trip on which he visited Kate (with Reynolds's sisters), in Emmitsburg. Eleanor Reynolds's letter to Captain McClure states, "When at Gettysburg in Nov. [1863], we were unable to ascertain its precise location [location of John's death] but that it will be identified there can be no doubt, Orderly Veil being very decided in his recollection of it, & all its surroundings." This seems to indicate that as of the date of this letter, February 16, 1864, the Reynolds sisters had not yet located the site with Veil. Veil's letter to Holzworth states, "I was on the field, *the following spring* with the Genls [*sic*] sisters, and located the identical spot" [emphasis added]. Also, in his memoirs Veil indicates that his early 1864 visit to Gettysburg and Emmitsburg, with Reynolds's sisters (at least two, likely Jane and Eleanor), came after he visited with the secretary of war in Washington, D.C., to discuss his promotion.

175. Reynolds Family Papers, Letters, Eleanor Reynolds to Charles Veil, June 5, 1865; August 7, 1865; October 9, 1865; January 15, 1866; August 6, 1866; August 9, 1866; January 15, 1867; and August 11, 1868, copies of original letters and transcriptions [hereafter RFP, Letters, E. Reynolds to C. Veil]; Courtesy of the Charles Henry Veil Family Papers, MS-60, Sharlot Hall Museum Library and Archives, copies of transcriptions of original letters (Sharlot Hall Museum holds the original letters) from Eleanor Reynolds to Charles Veil dated June 5, 1865; August 7, 1865; October 9, 1865; January 15, 1866; August 6, 1866; August 9, 1866; January 15, 1867; and August 11, 1868 [hereafter Letters, Sharlot Hall Collection]; secondary transcription excerpts of the aforementioned letters from various sources, as follows: Anderson, "Girl He Left Behind," 52–53; Veil, *Memoirs*, xvi–xvii.

176. Veil, *Memoirs*, xviii, 30. The editor of Veil's memoirs (Herman J. Viola) explains that Eleanor, on December 23, 1863, "met personally with President Lincoln to urge Veil's appointment as a second lieutenant in a regular army regiment." Apparently, her efforts were, at least in part, responsible for Veil's ensuing promotion, as Viola indicates Veil thanked the family for his commission in a letter dated January 5, 1864, and that Eleanor wrote to President Lincoln on January 11, 1864, thanking him for his "assistance" in "procuring" Veil's commission.

177. Daughters of Charity Provincial Archives, "Kate Hewitt and John Reynolds," https://docarchivesblog.org/about/; Reynolds Family Papers, Letters, Eleanor Reynolds to Charles Veil; Letters, Sharlot Hall Collection, August 7, 1865; Veil, *Memoirs*, xvi–xvii; Anderson, "Girl He Left Behind," 53. It is important to note that the Daughters of Charity is considered a "community," not an "order." DoC terminology is quite

different from that of other Catholic communities or orders. Per a Daughters of Charity internet post, "In other religious communities, this state of formation is called 'novitiate' and sisters in this stage are called 'novices.' In the Daughters of Charity, this stage of formation is called the Seminary and Sisters at this state are called Seminary Sisters." Also per this post, "Approximately 5 years after her vocation date, a Daughter of Charity (Sister) pronounces vows for the first time and renews them every year after that." Instead of being referred to as "nuns," as in other Catholic religious communities or orders, Daughters of Charity members are called "Sisters" and are expressly not known as "nuns." Also, per email correspondence with Sister Betty Ann McNeil, Vincentian scholar-in-residence, Division of Mission and Ministry, DePaul University (June 22 and 23, 2020), in the Daughters of Charity, the Sisters take "vows," not "final vows," after first being a Seminary Sister, then receiving the habit and a community name (such as Sister Hildegardis). Once they have been with the community for approximately five years, they "made" (not "pronounced") "vows" and then they would renew their "vows" each year thereafter on the Feast of the Annunciation, which is normally March 25 but can vary with the liturgical calendar.

178. RFP, Letters, E. Reynolds to C. Veil; Letters, Sharlot Hall Collection, June 5, and August 7, 1865; Veil, *Memoirs*, xvi; Anderson, "Girl He Left Behind," 53.

179. RFP, Letters, E. Reynolds to C. Veil; Letters, Sharlot Hall Collection, October 9, 1865, and January 15, 1866; Veil, *Memoirs*, xvi–xvii; Anderson, "Girl He Left Behind," 53.

17. Kate: The Daughters of Charity—Albany

180. George Rogers Howell and Jonathan Tenney, *Bi-Centennial History of Albany: History of the County of Albany, N.Y., from 1609 to 1866* (New York: W.W. Munsell & Co., 1886), section on "St. Joseph's Church," 755–56. St. Mary's and St. John's predated St. Joseph's.

181. Howell and Tenny, *Bi-Centennial History*, 755–56. This astonishing edifice still stands but is in a terrible state of disrepair and no longer serves as a house of worship.

182. Howell and Tenny, *Bi-Centennial History*, 755–56; Sister Delphine Steele, *History Albany, St. Mary's, St. Vincent's, St. Francis de Sales 1828–1955*, St. Joseph's School Collection, Box 1, Folder 4, Daughters of Charity Archives, Province of St. Louis, Emmitsburg, Maryland [hereafter Sister Delphine, *History*]; *St. Joseph's School, Albany, NY*, RG 11-4-2, Albany NY, St. Joseph's School Collection, Box 1, Folder 4, Daughters of Charity

Archives, Province of St. Louis, Emmitsburg, Maryland [hereafter *St. Joseph's School*]. Unfortunately, neither the building that housed the school or the teachers' residence at 261 North Pearl survives. The current buildings at those locations were built around the turn of the twentieth century.

183. Sister Delphine, *History Albany*; *St. Joseph's School*.

184. RFP, Letters, E. Reynolds to C. Veil; Letters, Sharlot Hall Collection, August 6, 1866, and August 9, 1866; Anderson, "Girl He Left Behind," 53. Transcription sources for the letters from Eleanor to Veil vary, in certain instances, for certain words and/or missing words. Here, the most logical words provided by the various sources are included in brackets, whenever a discrepancy, implied or missing word was noted among the transcriptions.

185. RFP, Letters, E. Reynolds to C. Veil; Letters, Sharlot Hall Collection, January 15, 1867; Anderson, "Girl He Left Behind," 53.

186. RFP, Letters, E. Reynolds to C. Veil; Letters, Sharlot Hall Collection, August 11, 1868; Veil, Memoirs, xvii; Anderson, "Girl He Left Behind," 53.

187. RFP, Letters, E. Reynolds to C. Veil; Letters, Sharlot Hall Collection, August 11, 1868; Veil, Memoirs, xvii; Anderson, "Girl He Left Behind," 53.

188. Marian Latimer, *"Is She Kate?": The Woman Major General John Fulton Reynolds Left Behind*, edited by Bernadette Loeffel Atkins (Gettysburg, PA: Farnsworth Military Impressions, 2005), 25; Council Minutes, August 31, 1868, Daughters of Charity Archives, Province of St. Louise, Emmitsburg, Maryland [hereafter DoC Council Minutes]. There has been some confusion about where Kate Hewitt was when she left the Daughters of Charity community. This stems from the fact that one source document at the Daughters of Charity Archives, DoC Admissions Book, indicates she left from the "Central House" at St. Joseph's School in Albany on "Sept. 3rd, 1868" while another Daughters of Charity source document, Daughters of Charity Catalogue (Admissions), 1809–1890, RG 13-0, indicates she left from "St. Vincent's House, Philadelphia" on "September 3rd, 1868." Of course, she couldn't have been two places at once, thus there is an error. It appears this mistake in the documentation is due to the fact that there was a St. Vincent's House in Philadelphia while the Central House in Albany was in the very building once known as St. Vincent's Orphanage. It appears whoever recorded the Philadelphia location did so in error. Kate Hewitt almost certainly left the Daughters of Charity from Albany, not Philadelphia.

18. Kate: Marriage

189. "Top 100 Biggest US Cities by Population," biggestuscities.com; Albany, New York, albanyny.gov; Discover Albany, albany.org.
190. New York Land Records, 1680–1975, familysearch.org; "Select School for Young Ladies," *Albany (NY) Evening Journal*, December 10, 1868; "Select School," *Daily Albany (NY) Argus*, August 20, 1869; "Dissolution," *Albany (NY) Evening Journal*, June 29, 1871; "Select School," *Albany (NY) Evening Journal*, August 21, 1871; "Select School Miss C. M. Hewitt," *Daily Albany (NY) Argus*, August 1, 1872; *Albany City Directory*, 1873, 104; DoC Council Minutes, March 20, 1869.
191. *Daily Albany Argus*, December 27, 1872; "Miss Hewitt's School," *Daily Albany Argus*, June 20, 1874.
192. Pfordt Family Bible; "Married," *Daily Albany Argus*, June 26, 1874; *Saint Joseph Albany, New York, Marriages H–Z, June 1843 to 1992* (Manchester, NH: American-Canadian Genealogical Society, 2013), repertoire number RP152 and the library call number, NY001-18 & 19; Harding and Pitkin, "Finding Kate," 56–63; original marriage record for Joseph B. Pfordt and Catherine M. Hewitt, from Saint Joseph's church archives, Albany, New York (record held at Sacred Heart, Albany, New York). Per the original marriage record, Reverend Thomas M. A. Burke, pastor of Saint Joseph's at the time, officiated.
193. *Albany City Directory*, New York, 1875, 184.

19. Kate: A Remarkable Legacy

194. Florence Griswold Museum, "Stitching It Together," https:// florencegriswoldmuseum.org/visit/families/stitching-it-together/; *United States Centennial Commission, International Exhibition 1876, Reports and Awards*, vol. 5, group 8, edited by Francis A. Walker, Chief of the Bureau of Awards (Philadelphia: J. B. Lippincott & Co., 1877–78), 54.
195. Veil, *Memoirs*, 34–36.
196. *Albany Evening Journal*, October 5, 1871; *Daily Albany Argus*, October 5, 1871.
197. "An Elegant Banner," *Daily Albany Argus*, July 23, 1875.
198. Kimberly Orcutt, *Power and Prosperity: American Art at Philadelphia's 1876 Centennial Exhibition* (University Park: Penn State University Press, 2017), 1–2.
199. "Centennial," *Chicago Tribune*, May 16, 1876.
200. "An Albany Women's Work," *Albany Evening Journal*, April 15, 1876; CPI Inflation Calculator.
201. Linda P. Gross and Theresa R. Snyder, Images of America: *Philadelphia's 1876 Centennial Exhibition* (Charleston, SC: Arcadia Publishing, 2005), 109–11.

202. Unfortunately, it appears both the St. Jean Baptiste Society banner and the Centennial Exhibition banner have been lost to history. Despite an exhaustive search, no evidence of either banner being extant can be found, nor has a photo or drawing showing either banner's appearance been located.

203. "Death of an Estimable Lady," *Daily Albany Argus*, October 7, 1876; "Death of Mrs. Pfordt," *Daily Albany Argus*, October 9, 1876; Interment Book, St. Agnes Cemetery, Menards, Albany, New York.

204. "Death of Mrs. Pfordt"; *Owego Gazette*, October 12, 1876.

205. "Death of an Estimable Lady"; "Death of Mrs. Pfordt." It was originally believed Kate may have been buried in a church cemetery in Albany and then moved to St. Agnes Cemetery as this was often the case with other individuals at the time. But this author's research indicates that Joseph purchased the family burial lot at St. Agnes on October 7, 1876, the day after Kate died and the day before she was buried (see Troy Irish Genealogy Society, St. Agnes Cemetery, Menands, NY, Lot Sale Book 1867–1922, sites.rootsweb.com). So she was not moved, but unfortunately extant records do not indicate which grave within the lot that Kate rests in.

206. "Death of Mrs. Pfordt"; *New York Herald*, October 7, 1876; *United States Centennial Commission, International*, 54.

20. John and Kate: Reflections

207. Haskell, *Battle of Gettysburg*, 14.

208. Information pertaining to the captions for this and the other Reynolds memorials, monuments and markers presented here is derived from: Wayne Craven, *The Sculptures at Gettysburg* (New York: Eastern Acorn Press & Monument Association, 1982), 28, 52, 55–57; Frederick W. Hawthorne, *Gettysburg: Stories of Men and Monuments as Told by Battlefield Guides* (Gettysburg and Hanover, PA: Association of Licensed Battlefield Guides and Sheridan Press, 1988), 19, 82, 135; Kalina Ingham Hintz, "'Dinna Forget': The Gettysburg Monuments to General John F. Reynolds," *Gettysburg Magazine*, January, 2005, 94–111.

ABOUT THE AUTHOR

Harding Collection.

Jeffrey J. Harding currently works as a licensed battlefield guide at Gettysburg National Military Park, freelance historian, leadership consultant and motivational speaker. Nearly a decade ago, Jeff retired from a thirty-three-year career as a civilian employee of the Department of the Navy where, among other things, he specialized in developing leadership programs based on the navy's greatest heroes, such as Fleet Admiral (FADM) Chester W. Nimitz. A recipient of the Department of the Navy's Meritorious Civilian Service Award, Jeff also received the prestigious honor of being inducted into his command's Hall of Fame. Over the past decade, Jeff has joined with numerous others in a number of sleuthing efforts to resolve mysteries of historical significance. In one instance, Jeff initiated the successful quest to locate a pen once used by Admiral Nimitz to sign the Japanese Instruments of Surrender—a pen that had gone "missing" since the end of the war. In another instance, Jeff discovered previously unused primary source weather observation data recorded at the time of the Battle of Gettysburg that allowed him and his colleague, meteorologist Dr. Jon Nese, to reveal something historians had been unable to determine since the battle—what the weather felt like to the soldiers during the battle. Most recently, Jeff spearheaded an effort with genealogist Mary Stanford Pitkin aimed at discovering the true fate of General John Reynolds's fiancée,

Catherine "Kate" Mary Hewitt—a mystery that had puzzled historians for over a century and a half. This book builds on that effort by detailing Kate Hewitt's entire life story alongside a fresh look at the life and military career of John Reynolds. Jeff's previously published works grace the pages of noted publications such as *Civil War Times, Naval History Magazine, Gettysburg Magazine*, the *Washington Times* and *The Gettysburg Experience*. Jeff has also conducted webinars and podcasts, appeared on The Weather Channel and Penn State's *Weather World* and was honored to speak at a special event held on the Battleship Missouri Memorial commemorating the sixty-eighth anniversary of the end of World War II. Jeff counts among his greatest honors as a guide once hosting the commanding officer and crew of the USS *Gettysburg* for a tour of the battlefield at Gettysburg. Jeff also considers himself as truly blessed to have participated as a volunteer with the Honor Flight organization, where he has had the distinct honor of meeting and accompanying so many of our nation's heroes who served in World War II, Korea and Vietnam as they visited their respective monuments in Washington, D.C.